New Life Story

By
Jessica Ramirez

Unless otherwise indicated, all scripture quotes are taken from the *New American Standard* Version of the Bible

ISBN is 1452886369 and EAN-13 is 9781452886367.

Copyright © 2010 by Jessica Ramirez

Printed in the United States of America.
All rights reserved under International Copyright Law. Contents and/or cover may not be reproduced in whole or in part without the express permission of the Author.

Having known Rhon and Jessica Ramirez for nearly 30 years as their Pastor and friend, this story takes on a special meaning. Jessica allows you the opportunity to view candidly into her life as she grows up and encounters a relationship with Jesus as her Lord and Master. My close relationship with Jessica, which includes traveling together, being in their home regularly and serving with them on our church board, allows me the liberty to say that the story you are about to read is genuine, not perfect but real as life gets. From my perspective, Jessica Ramirez is a shining example of God's Grace at work in a person's life. I believe you will be encouraged by the honest display of God's handiwork in the life of a "real" person.

Reverend James B. Holder

This book is dedicated to my Father, the real author of this story as well as to my wonderful husband, Rhon, for allowing me to share a part of his life along with mine, and to Andy, Jennifer and Ernie, Chris and Erica, and grandsons Drake, Jener, Philip and Judah. Oh, how I love you all!

I would also like to thank my church, New Life Center, and Pastor James and Brenda Holder for years of nurturing, encouraging and allowing me to be used of God.

Very special thanks go as well to Sandi Campbell, where would I be without you in my life?

A big thank you goes also to Gayle DiGiovanni for endless hours of reading and editing.

And to my prayer partners in this endeavor, Mary Read and Barbara Killian, all my wonderful New Life Center ladies and Kathy Key and Bonnie McPhail who my Father strategically placed in my life just when I thought this book might never be published.

Chapter 1
Searched and Known

"O LORD, You have searched me and known me. You know when I sit down and when I rise up; You understand my thought from afar." (Psalm 139:1-2)

As a child I was painfully lonely, terribly awkward, and for oh so many reasons I believed that I was glaringly different from my peers. In addition, I seemed to possess an uncanny, chameleon-like ability to both disappear into the woodwork and stick out like a huge and cumbersomely bandaged sore thumb! Of course, I had no control over either of these occurrences because more often than not I felt completely invisible when I desperately wanted to be noticed, yet was far too visible when complete obscurity would have been preferred. As a result, almost everything I've done, especially before committing my life to the Lord has been motivated to some degree by at least one, if not all, of those factors.

I wasn't a very cute little girl, I have pictures to prove it, and I wasn't a very nice one either. I'm afraid I was well into equally not very nice adulthood before I had the slightest idea of who, what or why I even existed. The sad reality is that I was a desperate and often very confused daughter who, was always loved, yet never considered the love of my family to be enough. Sadly, I gave much more consideration to what was missing from my life than to the wealth of blessings that had been lavished upon me. Seeds of self doubt, anger, confusion and insecurity began to take deep root in my heart when I was very young.

My youth was so fraught with bad choices and wrongdoing that I once considered rewriting my story into a fictional tale about a girl who was tempted by sin and rebellion yet always managed to make the right choice just before stepping completely out of bounds. I certainly would have included elements of my own past in the story but the fictional 'me' would have been much smarter, more confident, and most certainly more mature.

Except for a few, mostly meaningless, childish indiscretions the heroine of my tale would have grown up about twenty years earlier and come through the growing up process almost entirely unscathed; just wiser. But after years of prayerfully seeking the Lord I have decided to tell the real, and sometimes very painful, truth of how He brought me miraculously through less than ideal life circumstances as well as my own self-induced hardships and difficult situations. This is not a fairy tale, it is my own very personal story; some of which I'd much rather have kept in the woodwork. But I gladly declare that this is a real life Psalm 139 story if ever there was one. To God be the Glory!

I suppose now that I know my Creator has thoroughly searched my heart and my motives and has known all about me from even before my life began that I should feel indescribable shame. But I'm long past shame and regret and I now embrace the knowledge of His searching and knowing and all it implies with great joy. I am simply in awe of the fact that my Heavenly Father knows everything about me; my every ugly thought as well as my every thoughtless and sinful act and yet continues to love me and nurture me even with that incredible knowledge.

Before I knew Him I consistently rose up in rebellion when I should have waited quietly and I often sat stubbornly when I should have stepped out in obedience. He saw it all yet has provided me with a testimony that I know I can't keep to myself because it's really His story, not mine. I'm just the ghostwriter, my Heavenly Father is the author and finisher of my story and my life as well as my faith and now I gladly share all He's done for me.

Like many daughters, my mother's story is so inextricably part of mine I feel it's necessary to tell some of her story before I delve too deeply into my own. Doing so will explain a lot about why I felt the way I did about myself as well as why I made some of the choices I made, particularly as an adolescent and young adult. I certainly don't blame my mother for the many poor decisions I made nor do I even blame her for my lack of self worth. I do believe though, that situations and circumstances in both our lives played such a big part in the forming of our personalities, so different yet so much alike, that she cannot be ignored.

The best way I can describe my mother is to say that she was a very complicated woman with many fine qualities and truly a lady with the highest moral values. She was strong and independent, passionate about the things that were important to her, smart, modest, honest (often to a fault), thrifty and practical. My mother was also a swift and stern disciplinarian, often angry, judgmental, unforgiving, and negative; her glass seemed always to be at least two thirds empty. She didn't easily trust or give others the benefit of the doubt. Reserved and extremely private she was not a 'people person', in fact she was truly a loner; yet in spite of her wariness of others she was often a poor judge of character, judging people far too often by their appearance alone.

As my mother aged she also grew fearful, often battled depression and in her later years became almost a recluse. Yet as far back as I can remember most everyone who knew her, as well as anyone could ever know my mother, found her warm, gracious and charming, and she certainly had the ability to be all those things, but even the few she considered friends were usually kept at arm's length. There was a sense of sadness and loneliness about her that seemed to hang over her like a cloud, yet she fiercely denied being lonely. She admitted to feeling awkward and inadequate, even into her later years, but above all else I just thought she was odd. I didn't appreciate my mother for the unique and special individual she was and in many ways she did march to a different drummer. How could I ever be anything but different as well?

My mother, whose given name was Naomi, was the youngest of four children and in her later years she confided on more than one occasion that she'd felt very unloved and unwanted as a child. My mother's siblings included a brother, my Uncle Joe, who was almost twelve years older, a sister, about eight years older and another brother, Murray, who was just four years older. It was my grandmother's relationship with Murray that contributed so much to my mother's insecurities as a child. She insisted to her dying day that Murray was my grandmother's favorite child and even though he was apparently unmerciful to his little sister (as older brothers often are) in my grandmother's eyes it seemed he could do no wrong. A few of the stories I've heard from their childhood might have been quite humorous if my mother hadn't been so emotionally hurt by his antics. Ultimately Murray ran away from home when he was just fourteen years old, understandably causing his parents a great deal of heartache and concern. I'm sure this fact contributed even further to my mother's sense of neglect. Sadly, my mother harbored ill feelings toward Murray throughout their lives and the two of them were never close.

My grandfather was a farmer but my grandmother wanted her children to have advantages she felt only city life could afford them so on several occasions she moved with her children to either Muskogee or Tulsa leaving her husband behind to tend the farm. I've always suspected that theirs was not a happy marriage because when my grandmother did live on the farm my poor grandfather resided in the chicken house! (As I remember the chicken house wasn't that large, either, but at least it was much bigger than a dog house.)

My grandfather was of Scotch-Irish descent, my grandmother was one quarter Creek Indian and for some reason I've always felt that combination might be a volatile one, at least it was so for them. My mother told of being subjected to many an argument as a child and I'm quite certain that being separated so frequently from her father, whom she adored, was a factor that added to her insecurities and negative feelings about her childhood. I believe my mother grew to resent her mother for keeping her from her father so much of the time.

It was my mother's sister, my Aunt Thyra who became my mother's savior during her childhood and her ultimate lifelong best friend. They had a close and loving relationship and as a young child my aunt looked after my mother while my grandmother did whatever she could to help provide extra household income. For a time my grandmother made and sold homemade bread and Aunt Thyra delivered the bread in a wagon with my mother in tow. I can just picture, Norman Rockwell style, a little girl of about ten or twelve pulling a wagon containing a little sister barely visible beneath loaves of homemade bread. If I close my eyes I can almost smell the fresh bread, feel a warm summer breeze and see the cracks in the tree lined sidewalks.

One of the truly selfless and remarkable things that Aunt Thyra did for her younger sister was to buy a piano for her and provide her with piano lessons. My mother actually became a very accomplished pianist and though she didn't talk much about this part of her life, for years she would play the piano almost every day, playing with such feeling she would often become lost in her music. One of my happiest memories from early childhood is of dancing around the room with tireless joy and complete abandon as my mother played.

My mother was also fiercely patriotic and joined the Waves, the women's branch of the Navy during World War II. In doing so, I believe she gave up an opportunity to further her talent, possibly even the fulfillment of her dream of becoming a concert pianist in order to serve her country. One of the few mementos that she had kept from her own childhood was the printed program for a recital that her piano teacher had arranged for her to display her talents. There had even been a guest violinist that accompanied my mother on a few of the pieces. The program was impressive and though my mother never would have admitted it I believe the recital was a very big deal. My mother was truly gifted but her feelings of being unloved and unwanted likely played a big part in keeping her from having the self confidence she needed to realize all that for which she had been so fearfully and wonderfully made.

My mother's tour of duty in the Waves eventually took her to New York City where she remained after her discharge from the service. This was her one big adventure, she loved New York City and I suspect she also enjoyed the independence she experienced working there and living on her own. She certainly had fond memories of her life there and once during a conversation with my husband she revealed that she had met my father on the steps of the library in New York City. I was delighted to hear anything about their meeting because I don't know very much about my father at all. She'd never told me anything about their meeting and I was a little surprised she'd told Rhonnie.

The story of their meeting was certainly a big surprise to me because my mother was always so prim and proper, even to the point of being a little socially backward that I can't even in my wildest imagination (and I have a really wild imagination) see her getting 'picked up' by anyone. I also understand that my father was equally as straight-laced; go figure! (I like to think that is just one of the many elements of my own fearful and wonderful making.)

My father, who I believe may have worked for the CIA, (yes, really) was from New York and after my parents married they made their home in Flushing where I was born three years later. My parents were a little older than the average newlywed couple when they married and consequently older first time parents; my mother was thirty three and my father, forty three when I was born. I've never been given any reason to think my birth was anything other than a highly anticipated and miraculous event for both my parents. In fact, from every indication my life began in the most idyllic way possible; as a cherished, treasured and wanted child. I believe my parents planned to nurture and lovingly protect me to the very best of their abilities but the best of intentions and the happiest of families can be shattered in a literal heartbeat and in three short years that is exactly what would happen to mine.

I have four vague, almost ethereal memories of our family life in Flushing; the dearest, really more a sensation than a memory, is of my father lifting me high in the air, perhaps after returning home from a days work. I also remember once watching my father stand on a ladder to change a light bulb in the kitchen and my mother's attempt to show me an owl in a hollow tree outside our apartment. I don't remember actually seeing the owl and suspect that what impressed me about that incident was my mother's frustration in realizing that I probably didn't see what she was so intent on showing me.

Then there is my most vivid memory of New York; going into the bathroom of our apartment to find my father on the floor with my mother kneeling beside him, trying to prevent me from entering the room with one hand while holding desperately on to him with the other. I was three years old and in that moment my father, at the age of forty-six had just suffered a fatal heart attack.

I believe the impact of that tragedy upon my mother was so profound and painful that a large portion of her heart ceased to function that day as well. My mother would never remarry or even consider the possibility of doing so; as for me, it would be decades before I would fully process the event. That day my life was redefined and because there would never again be a father figure in our home it would take an incredible encounter with God for me to overcome my inability to relate to Him as my Heavenly Father and that encounter would not come for nearly forty long years.

After my father's death my mother brought me back to Oklahoma and my grandmother's wonderful old farmhouse; the house my grandfather had built on about seventy acres just north of Bixby in the 1920's. My grandfather had passed away shortly before I was born and by the time my mother and I arrived at the farm only twenty acres of the original property remained which was just enough to maintain an alfalfa crop.

I remember being absolutely intrigued with the modest white house with blue trim which must have seemed like a mansion after the confines of the tiny Flushing apartment. Even as a child I appreciated the fact that the house had history and character. I was fascinated by the discolored place on the ceiling in the kitchen where a rather large hole had been patched but never painted to match the rest of the ceiling. (My grandmother's sister had fallen through the floor of the unfinished attic years earlier.) I marveled at the two oak trees that had been planted by my grandfather decades before with the intention that a hammock would one day hang between them. I was intrigued by the large, old wooden telephone that hung on the wall of the big country kitchen; two short and one long ring meant that the call was for us, otherwise the rings went unanswered.

One of my favorite features in the house was a long closet that seemed to magically connect two bedrooms. One could enter the closet in one bedroom, work through the hanging clothes and exit the closet, almost Narnia style, into the other bedroom. I got into a little trouble one day when I was about six years old by hiding in that closet, taking full advantage of this wondrous feature and slipping back and forth from bedroom to bedroom while my grandmother looked frantically throughout the house and yard for me. As best I can remember that is the only time my grandmother ever scolded me because it had frightened her terribly when she couldn't find me.

But the very best things on the farm by far were the animals. There were no horses, cows or anything that might be considered 'farmish' but my grandmother had Baby, a beautiful, gentle collie, lots of chickens, and there was always at least one cat on the farm. To this day I adore cats of all breeds, shapes and sizes, as did my mother throughout her life! Oh yes, I think my grandmother might have been a little upset with me the day I dressed several of the chickens, the ones I could catch anyway, in doll clothes. Oh, the wonders of childhood!

My sweet, sweet grandmother, whom I called Granny, was almost seventy years old when we arrived on her doorstep. She was a strong, capable woman, a tireless worker and she absolutely doted on me; even as a small child I knew I was her pride and joy. I've never been able to fully understand my mother's feelings about her mother because my grandmother was never anything but completely loving to me; she seemed to exude warmth, patience and understanding. My grandmother became my lifeline and my rock and she provided me with a much needed sense of security during my early childhood.

My mother was a very hard worker as well and upon moving back to Oklahoma she immediately enrolled in secretarial school and took a job at Gulf Oil Corporation in Tulsa. Neither Granny nor my mother owned a car so for years my mother took the bus to work every day, about twenty miles one way, which made her workdays and her time away from home very lengthy. While my mother worked so hard to provide for us I was left in the daily care of my grandmother. I loved being on the farm with Granny but I missed my father terribly, or perhaps by now it was the idea of having a father that I missed, at any rate I believe that on some level I blamed my mother for the fact that my father was no longer with us, just as I realize now that she had blamed her mother for keeping her from her father. In addition, I saw so little of my mother that she and I began to grow distant from one another and her feelings were often hurt because I consistently wanted to be with my grandmother instead of with her. Now that I have children and grandchildren of my own I can't imagine how truly hurt she must have been by my withdrawal from her.

My mother (who absolutely insisted on being called Mother) and my grandmother argued frequently. My obvious preference for my grandmother probably fueled those bitter feelings my mother had harbored for so long. I seemed to relate best to my mother as the person who came home only to discipline me and then I would always run to my grandmother for comfort. In addition, I don't remember that my mother hugged or kissed me very often as a child and consequently as I got older affection between us seemed forced and was therefore infrequent. It was not in my mother's nature to be spontaneous or affectionate with others either and I suspect that is because her feelings toward her mother, as well as her insecurities, spilled over into all of her relationships.

I was about six or seven when I was introduced to television. One of the first shows I remember is *Father*

Knows Best and I was just captivated by this perfect, make believe, all-American family and everything it seemed to represent. From my limited vantage point *Father Knows Best* embodied an absolutely ideal, if not perfect world. You can imagine the impact even the title might have had on a little girl who so desperately longed for her own father. The Andersons of television were so warm and loving with each other and Margaret Anderson seemed to be the antithesis of my own mother. I made up my mind very early that I would one day have a *Father Knows Best* family, a normal family, not a peculiar one like my own.

Watching *Father Knows Best* I realized what a wonderful thing it would be to have siblings. My sense of loneliness was heightened as I became more and more aware that I didn't have any siblings and from that point forward I longed for a brother or sister to share my life with. My mother once told me that other children were never part of her plan so I also determined early on that I would have a houseful of children. It's surely ironic that my mother, one of four children, only wanted one child so she could expend all her energy making sure that one felt loved while I wanted three children, just like the Andersons, to insure that no one would ever be lonely.

In addition to the fact that there wasn't a brother or sister to share my life with, I had yet to meet the cousins that were close to my age, and there were no neighbors to speak of, at least none with children. I really only knew how to communicate with adults and even my encounters with adults were limited on the farm. Uncle Joe came regularly to bring groceries or see about a repair but he usually kept his distance from me. Hardly anyone else that I knew, except Aunt Thyra, visited and she visited often and her visits were usually punctuated with some kind of special treat.

I longed for someone my own age to play with but since we were fairly isolated on the farm and had no car, play dates with other children were extremely rare so, out of necessity, I learned to cultivate a very active imagination. I talked to myself incessantly and I created an imaginary friend I called Pamela George. I surely didn't lack for dolls and toys and I had all kinds of child sized playthings. I loved all things domestic and I would play house and talk to my dolls, and Pamela George, for hours on end, I even had an imaginary husband on occasion – I think I may have even called him George. All practice for that *Father Knows Best* future that surely awaited me.

For a special treat my grandmother and I would take occasional trips by bus into Tulsa to have lunch with Mother and Aunt Thyra. In those days the streets of downtown Tulsa were lined with wonderful places to shop; like Brown-Dunkin, Vandevers and Seidenbachs, to name a few. After lunch Granny and I would shop for toiletries or fabric until my mother was ready to leave work for the day, then the three of us would ride the bus home together. Granny and I would get all dressed up for these occasions and they were special events indeed.

In those days the bus stopped wherever anyone stood along the road waiting for it. One morning as we attempted to board the bus right in front of the farm house my grandmother must have looked down as she took that first step up and onto the bus. Shrieking, she suddenly grabbed my hand and very quickly we both made a beeline to the house as my flustered grandmother waived the bus on. Dressed to the nines from her stylish, black pillbox hat to her sensible but smart shoes Granny had, of all things, forgotten to put on her skirt! Yes, she had been standing on South Memorial, waiting for the bus in a ruffled white blouse complete with brooch and a lacy white slip! The memory of that makes me laugh to this day because even though it embarrassed my grandmother considerably we would all laugh about that ill-fated shopping trip many times in the years to come.

I'm so thankful for Granny, who surely added a sense of balance and stability to our lives. I really don't believe my mother could have managed without her, a fact that I'm sure my mother found both a source of deep gratitude and equally great resentment. The most outstanding thing that I remember about my grandmother is that hers was the first Christian influence in my life and for that influence I am ever so grateful. It is because of my grandmother that we went to church at all and we went, all three of us, every time the doors were open. Granny would take me along to her occasional ladies meetings and I have a very vivid picture in my mind of her reading her Bible daily to the very end of her life. I remember seeing her fill a cracker box with food for a hungry man who had come to our doorstep one day and I'm sure she did this more than once.

She belonged to a little church that had its beginnings in an old motel and for a year or two church services were held in the largest room of that motel, the former bar. Once during an evening service two very inebriated men staggered into the place only to stagger back out very quickly when they discovered that their old hangout was now a house of worship! (I guess that would be a 'sobering' experience.) The guest rooms were used as Sunday school classrooms and I learned John 3:16 and "Jesus Loves Me" in those little rooms and even though it would be many years before I would commit my life to the Lord I surely know that numerous seeds were planted in my heart during that time.

During another Sunday evening church service when I was about six years old, my mother responded to an altar call and I followed along after her though I had no idea where she was going or why. (I'd probably been sleeping on the pew just minutes before.) Surely an altar worker must have talked to me that night because later that evening my grandmother was so excited that I had asked

Jesus into my heart. I, of course, assumed because of her excitement that I had done just that even though I really didn't have any idea what that might have entailed. After that evening my mother did become quite active in the church, seeming to jump in with both feet. She played the piano during church services and taught a Sunday school class but if memory serves me correctly, and I'm afraid it does in this regard, neither of our lives produced any real fruit after that night.

As you might well imagine, the memory of my sweet grandmother's love for her Lord and her example of faithfulness makes it even more difficult for me to comprehend my mother's sense of not being loved by this woman but if there is anything that my own life story has taught me it is that people can and do change when they commit their lives fully to the Lord. "Therefore if anyone is in Christ, he is a new creature; the old things passed away; behold, new things have come." (2 Corinthians 5:17). I truly believe that whatever work the Lord had done in my grandmother over the years was a complete work! Whatever had happened in the past that hurt my mother so deeply just didn't seem to be a part of the grandmother that I knew yet even after her own salvation experience my mother held tightly to her pain from the past.

Living on my grandmother's farm I was as secure and happy as I could be given my particular circumstances and Mother, Granny and Aunt Thyra sought to provide me with as many life enriching experiences as they could. The four of us took yearly vacations going to such magnificent places as the Grand Canyon, Carlsbad Caverns – a place I still especially love – the Teton Mountains, Yosemite, Sequoyah, Mesa Verde and Yellowstone National Parks. I still love vacations, specifically road trips, taking time along the way so that nothing is overlooked because that's the way I learned to vacation as a child. One of my mother's most endearing qualities was that she loved to take the time to soak up every experience that she had and whether she was at an art gallery or just gazing at a sunset she always took time to smell the roses.

The three of them also exposed me to as many ballets, symphonies and operas as they could possibly squeeze into my little world so I learned to love the performing arts, yes, even opera, as a very young child. Music was always an outlet for my mother and she would often be so moved by it that she would openly sob. Mother was not an easy crier and she rarely let her guard down yet crying over an orchestral performance or an opera was apparently a safer, more acceptable expression of emotion for her than tears shed over the most devastating loss she would ever suffer. This is one of several areas where I absolutely did not and could not follow in her footsteps. I know that my tear collection (Psalm 56:8) occupies a substantially large bottle in heaven. I even cried when I went to see the movies *Toy Story* and *Monster's Inc.*, for 'crying' out loud!

I do fully understand how certain experiences that deeply affect us can cause emotion to flood over us when we least expect it. When our youngest child was seven years old I suffered one of several miscarriages. A few weeks later I took him to see the animated movie, *The Land Before Time* and was absolutely horrified when one of the main characters, a mother dinosaur, died as her little one looked on begging his mother to get up. I cried my eyes out as a flood of grief and a sense of loss swept over me. We had to wait until the theater was completely empty before we were able to get up from our seats and walk out.

In the early 50's the Bixby school system was small and though I don't remember that I had any really close friends I did have an occasional playmate once I began attending school. Everyone in Bixby knew me because everyone knew and respected my grandmother and Uncle Joe. I still remember the names of some of my teachers in

Bixby and I remember learning to read and how my teacher just cheered when it all 'clicked' for me. In addition to the security I felt living in a small community I also completely enjoyed my status as the 'family baby'. Due to divorce Uncle Joe had been estranged for several years from his two children, who were now in their twenties, both married and with children of their own that were by now nearly my age; perhaps that is why he preferred to keep me at a distance.

    Granny had not seen Uncles Joe's children in a very long time and I had never even met them. Uncle Murray had only one child, a daughter who was about twelve years old when I was born, they didn't live close by so my grandmother didn't have the opportunity to see her as often as she would have liked either; I, on the other hand, was joined to her at the hip. My Aunt Thyra, who lived in Tulsa, never married and that is why on her frequent visits she spoiled me rotten, always bringing gifts and making sure I had my favorite foods.

    In spite of the loneliness the days spent on the farm were simple, peaceful and wonderful and they are days I will always look back on with complete nostalgia. Sadly I have no pictures from those days but if I could capture one childhood memory in a photograph it would be a picture of a little girl in the swing that hung from a pecan tree in the front yard. There would be a bright blue sky overhead, soft pink and yellow lantana by the porch and Granny would be hanging laundry on the nearby clothesline. Baby would be dutifully close by. If I close my eyes I can feel the warmth of the sun, smell the clean clothes and see the white house, the rock cellar, the barn and the chicken house as clearly as if I were sitting in that swing today.

    In committing these memories to paper, some very painful to recall while others quite wonderful, I am provoked by this question; was my childhood really as difficult as I remember it? The answer would have to be both yes and no. Adolescence would certainly have been much easier if I had been more compliant and I have surely come to understand, and accept, that so much of what I once perceived as difficult may have been the result of my own doing. My mother was often hard to please and our relationship, like hers with her mother was difficult as well and I often pushed her to the limit. I also realize that perhaps my perception of certain events may have become exaggerated, even a little distorted over time.

All things considered, those early years were, for the most part, very good ones. I've come to realize that some of what I remember as painful or unfair makes so much more sense to me looking back with grown up eyes. I certainly would not wish a willful child like myself on anyone and I now know how incredibly challenging raising a child is for two committed and knowledgeable parents. I also know that attempting to raise a child without the help of the Lord, either singly or as a couple is a recipe for disaster! I fully acknowledge that my mother had her work cut out for her!

Although I have bittersweet memories of my early childhood I cherish the memory of the farm and the simplicity of those days. It now seems ironic that my recurring thought during those carefree and seemingly endless days was that I would never grow old like my grandmother. I think I must have believed that she was born aged and that I would always remain a child, partly because in those days one day truly seemed just like another. The years seemed to pass so slowly and for some reason that is lost on me now, I actually wished time would go by a little faster; especially when Christmas or my birthday was approaching.

Now, my mental picture of the little girl in the swing almost takes my breath away because that window of childhood joy and abandon and all those truly special days that seemed to stand still in time, seems so brief and the picture completely belies the events that would soon overshadow its carefree serenity. Change was once again in the air for the little girl in the swing as another event that would further define who, what and why I was lay just around the corner and it would be a very unwelcome event indeed.

Yet my Heavenly Father would continue to search and know my every thought, dream and desire as well as my heartaches and the hateful feelings I often harbored in my heart. He would carefully watch my every behavior and even my most willful disobedience would not dampen His love or thwart His plan for me. Through the coming years He would continue to save my every tear and He would continue to make provision to one day fulfill my hearts deepest desire in a way that would be more than I could have ever imagined. He understood from afar the deep void that the death of my father had left in my life and He determined that He would one day fill it to overflowing.

Chapter 2
Intimately Acquainted

"You scrutinize my path and my lying down, and are intimately acquainted with all my ways. Even before there is a word on my tongue, behold, O LORD, You know it all." (Psalm 139:3-4)

I was nine years old when my mother came home from work one early summer day and announced that we would be moving to Oklahoma City. Gulf was transferring a large number of its employees there, including my mother's boss and she would be going dutifully along. I remember that I protested loudly but the plan had apparently already been etched in stone and the move was set in motion within a few weeks as my mother went on to Oklahoma City to settle into her new job and a temporary apartment. She would look for a house for us all to move into before the beginning of school in the fall. In the meantime Granny, who was now seventy five years old, decided it was time to sell the farm in order to move with us and I would finally get a taste of the true passage of time as that last summer on the farm passed entirely too quickly!

There would be huge, almost unfathomable, adjustments to be made and the day that the veterinarian came to the farm to put Baby to sleep along with a couple of kittens that I had become quite attached to still ranks up there among my life's most traumatic experiences. Though Baby was old and a country dog at heart I didn't, and frankly still don't, understand that extreme way of thinking. My mother loved animals and we always had at least one pet but she seemed to believe that it was better to have a pet, even a healthy one, put down than to give it away and apparently moving them to Oklahoma City was out of the question for reasons that completely escaped me. I don't think she even trusted the veterinarian to find the animals good homes and I never understood why Uncle Joe couldn't at least take Baby to his place. I must also mention that my mother was not entirely against the idea of euthanasia for human beings in some situations and even contemplated suicide on more than one occasion in her later years.

I faced another huge adjustment when my mother and I had to leave my grandmother in Bixby to complete the business of selling the farm while we moved on to Oklahoma City because school would begin in a few days. On the day my mother and I arrived at the shabby, dark house that she'd rented there was a huge dead tarantula awaiting us on the porch right at the threshold of the front door. It didn't matter to me one iota that it was dead - there couldn't have been a more formidable welcoming committee. I'd never seen a tarantula before and I was immediately terrified at the sight of it. That night I couldn't sleep in the unfamiliar room and I lay in bed absolutely petrified with fear (too frightened to even cry out) as I envisioned dozens of enormous and menacing tarantulas running rampant all over the house. Granny would be unable to join us for a few more weeks and I missed her terribly as I cried for her and grieved for Baby and for the lost kittens. I think I knew even before arriving in Oklahoma City that my life would again be forever changed and way down deep inside my nine year old mind I must have also known that the change would not be for the better.

Over the next few weeks I would cry often. I hated my new school and all of Oklahoma City in general. I longed to hear the sound of the hay baler at night, something that I would still love to hear again. I would frequently be lulled to sleep by that sound on the farm as the workmen would sometimes work well after dark to finish the job of harvesting the alfalfa crop. I suspect that my mother and grandmother missed the farm too and I wondered if my mother ever regretted the decision she'd made but I was too busy being hurt and angry to notice how anyone else was feeling. I didn't even have my own bedroom and for the next few years I would share a room with either my mother or my grandmother. When I entered my teen years I slept on a hide-a-bed in the living room.

The timing of our move to Oklahoma City happened to coincide with the height of my childhood awkwardness; fourth grade. I guess I hadn't realized how awkward I was before that time but having to adjust to a new school suddenly made me very aware of it. First of all I must say that my social skills, like my mothers, were just pitiful! I was skinny with bright red, frizzy and completely unmanageable hair. (I wanted desperately to be a blond when I was little.) Oh, and I almost forgot the best part. The very first day I ever attended school, way back in Bixby kindergarten, someone must have immediately realized that I couldn't see my nose in front of my face because I also had to wear glasses, rather thick ones, and I needed to wear them all the time. I am truly grateful that I was at least afforded the luxury of contact lenses in my teens.

Even through the myriad of difficult adjustments I did manage to make a couple of friends in fourth grade when thankfully, I discovered two other girls that were also new to my school. On the positive side, I was able to join the Brownies, I could walk the four blocks home from school everyday all by myself and I was allowed to take ballet lessons, something I had always wanted to do, probably as compensation for the trauma of the move. I would not have had that luxury in Bixby and I was occasionally reminded of that fact, and perhaps I needed reminding because I was undoubtedly developing an 'attitude' as I approached adolescence. It was also inevitable that I would take piano lessons and practice for a required hour every day except Sunday. That may have been my mother's attempt at living vicariously through me, all I know is that I didn't like piano lessons, yet now one of my biggest regrets is that I didn't appreciate them more.

But back to the issue of awkwardness; I discovered boys in fifth grade, especially one, who I'll call Richie, when he began attending my school mid-year. I knew little about relationships in general and boy-girl relationships in particular because I was really best at communicating with adults who more often than not let me take center stage. So, I proceeded to let the whole world know that I liked Richie and that I had decided, and likely announced to all who would listen, that he would be my boyfriend. One spring day during recess I literally chased Richie all around the playground and the more I chased the more obvious his dislike for me and his disdain for the chasing became.

By the time recess was over I was so hurt and angry that I stood on a chair behind the door waiting for Richie to enter the classroom. As soon as he came through the doorway I hit him as hard as I could on top of his head with a rather hefty textbook. First of all let me say that I am so very thankful that he wasn't badly hurt and the most puzzling thing about the incident is that I didn't get into very much trouble over it. The teacher did scold me and I think I may have even had to visit the principal's office but my mother never found out about it and whatever punishment I may have received at school was so minimal that I've forgotten it. It probably doesn't need to be said that Richie gave me a very wide berth from that day forward.

But by far, one of my most embarrassing and awkward elementary school moments occurred one day in the spring of my sixth grade year, right after lunch when sure enough, I discovered to my horror that I had started my first menstrual period. My mother had prepared me very, very well and in a completely factual and realistic way for this event and though I liked the idea of developing and wearing nail polish, lipstick and a bra it seemed that once I did begin to develop it all happened overnight and this part of it, well let me just say I was *not* ready for. I am truly grateful that my mother had prepared me so well for that day because even knowing what to expect I found the experience frightening.

On that ever so 'special' day I told my teacher what had just happened with as much calm and discretion as a twelve year old could muster and she immediately sent me home. I walked the four blocks home only to be sent right back to school after getting all 'fixed up' by my grandmother. When I reentered the classroom that afternoon my sweet little teacher (what *was* she thinking!) proudly announced to the whole world that "Jessica became a woman today." Definitely one of those moments that I truly wish I could have completely disappeared into the woodwork. Mercifully, the announcement seemed to go over the heads of the boys in the class and even most of the girls as well! Might I be so bold as to suggest that going to lunch or to the mall in 'celebration' of such a monumental occasion might be preferable to returning to school; at least for that one day, just to be on the safe side.

Then there was the inevitable transition to junior high school. I began seventh grade at what was in the 60's, one of Oklahoma City's more prestigious high schools and from the very first day everything seemed to go wrong. This was a large school and at that time included seventh to twelfth grades with all the classes contained in the same building. After having completed fourth through sixth grades at the same elementary school I was just beginning to settle in to my surroundings and though I only had one or two friends my age I was finally feeling a little better about the move. I had even succeeded in making a couple of friends on our street, both of whom were girls and both a year older than I was. Since they were older and more 'experienced' I actually believed, based upon what they had to say about it, that I would like seventh grade; either they were very wrong in their perceptions or I was very wrong to believe them.

Any excitement I might have felt about entering junior high completely vanished when all of a sudden I found myself lost in a huge building with hundreds of complete strangers from several different area elementary schools – and that was just seventh grade orientation day. When the actual first day of school arrived I realized how small I really was compared to the upperclassmen, many of whom would have just as easily stepped on a little awkward and bewildered seventh grader as to look at her, if in fact they had even seen her at all. Looking back I think my brain may have been very close to shutting down at the prospect of having six different teachers, traveling from class to class (without getting lost), the promised humiliation of gym class (a book in itself) and through it all it seems that I knew no one in any of my classes. Once again I would have to face the difficult and overwhelming task of making new friends.

I believe that it was at the very beginning of my seventh grade year that I became aware of just how different I was as I drifted invisibly from class to class to lunch and back to class again. Of course, the greatest reason I felt so different from my peers is because my mother was widowed and in the 50's and 60's one parent families were simply not usual occurrences. I recall knowing only three or four girls whose parents were divorced throughout all the years I was growing up. I certainly didn't know another soul, at least not in my age group, whose father had died! To this day I don't fully understand why I felt this way but the fact that my father had died and that I was being raised by my mother and grandmother was almost a source of embarrassment to me. It seemed that I was having to explain my situation more and more frequently as I got older yet I never got used to or comfortable with the explanation.

I often feared that all my 'differences' would stand out like that proverbial sore thumb yet I was, for the most part, unnoticed. The two girls from the neighborhood that had been my friends suddenly wanted nothing to do with me, at least not at school and since my two friends from grade school had none of the same classes I did we quickly grew apart. I was truly petrified throughout the year yet it never even occurred to me that many of the other seventh graders might have been experiencing some of the same fears and misgivings that I was dealing with. I wonder now how many of them felt lonely, awkward or different too. I also know now that feeling that way is probably more normal than not, especially at the beginning of seventh grade!

In addition to the staggering social adjustments, academics were suddenly much more difficult and though I had done reasonably well in elementary school where I had made mostly A's and B's I now found that learning, especially math concepts, was extremely difficult. To this day I'm afraid I'm not good at math. I also must acknowledge that I could have done better academically, even in grade school, had I tried just a little harder but I'm afraid that I had developed the habit early on of doing just what I needed to do in order to get by. Now, though, I was truly overwhelmed by the difficulty of the subjects, the amount of homework and the fact that now the teachers, for the most part, didn't seem to care about students they only saw for an hour a day. At least in elementary school the teachers had been loving and nurturing and they knew everyone by name almost immediately; of course it's easier to learn twenty-five names than a couple of hundred. In turn, I remember the names of only three of my teachers throughout high school; two of my seventh grade teaches because they were exceptionally sweet and caring and a male science teacher I had in tenth grade for a less than noble reason.

The one constant that remained a part of our lives was that my grandmother, my mother and I had been attending a church from the moment we moved to Oklahoma City, again because of Granny's faithfulness. My mother became the church pianist and taught a younger girls' Sunday school class for a short time after the move but for reasons that I never fully understood she very abruptly just stopped going to church altogether just about the time I entered junior high. She obviously had been hurt or offended in some way, though she would never say who had hurt her or how she'd been offended. Even though she would not be attending church anymore I was still required to go in order to please my grandmother and, I suspect to give my mother some time to herself.

Today the absolute highlight of my week is Sunday morning Sunday school and church for oh so many reasons; the corporate worship, the fellowship with my church family and our pastor's excellent sermons are just a few of them. And I can hardly wait to join a handful of prayer warriors for intercessory prayer during the Sunday school hour. I have to admit though that in those days I hated getting up on Sunday mornings and going to church while my mother stayed behind nicely ensconced in her robe and pajamas, but this was not a negotiable issue. I don't remember that I really complained too much about it (quite uncharacteristic for me) and I know now that there must have been something about my grandmother's fervor that ministered to me whether I realized it or not because I really was clueless concerning the Lord and His ways that are higher than mine. I had absolutely no relationship with Him nor did I have any desire for that relationship. My world, such as it was, revolved around me, at least in my mind, and many times I would grumble on my way out the door that when I was old enough to make my own decisions I would stay home on Sunday mornings to drink coffee and read the newspaper in my pajamas too.

I also think that part of the reason I never really argued with my mother about this issue is because I was starting to be aware that her stress level seemed to be steadily rising. I believe this may have started about the time of the move and now my mother would get angry about the smallest things. She would fly into a rage over something as insignificant as my picking up a dented can of green beans when we went to the grocery store. I just recently came to the realization that it was around the time of her decision to stop attending church that my mother completely stopped playing her beloved piano. I wonder now if anyone noticed how she was changing.

Naomi means 'pleasant' in Hebrew but my mother had become anything but. She chose instead to be angry, hurt and bitter and sadly, she would remain this way throughout most of the rest of her life. Though she was never called Mara, which means 'bitter', it seems she felt as Naomi, Ruth's mother-in-law must have felt after her husband had died leaving her alone. Because she had such a difficult childhood, and her husband had died leaving her alone to raise a willful child, with no choice but to return to the home she so wanted to leave behind, my mother might as well have said "Do not call me Naomi; call me Mara, for the Almighty has dealt very bitterly with me." (Ruth 1:20).

I now see that my mother was also becoming increasingly withdrawn and sullen when she was stressed or angry and I was beginning to dislike being around her more and more. I wonder if she might have been experiencing some of the symptoms of menopause, she'd had a hysterectomy a few years earlier but menopause would certainly explain some of her behavior; it wouldn't explain the fact that this behavior went on for about thirty years, I certainly would hope not anyway. I believe it is more likely that her moodiness intensified once she made the decision to leave the church because she had also turned her back completely on the Lord and had opened herself up to whatever the devil wanted to pour in.

Her only social life had been through church activities and as she became more and more reclusive I began to feel a greater sense of isolation myself even though we lived in the middle of a sprawling city. In addition, her behavior caused me to be even more aware of my differences because other mothers seemed so outgoing, cheerful and involved in their children's activities. I think I must have realized even then that my mother may not have been emotionally healthy. My mother was very much like Claudie, the beautiful silvery gray cat that Rhonnie and I had for many years. Claudie would absolutely delight in being stroked until she'd had enough and in an instant she would quickly jump up, bite at us and run away. At least the cat was somewhat predictable. I never knew when my mother would suddenly turn from being relaxed and cordial to angry and insufferable.

I believe that I would have done anything to keep from feeling left out and I craved attention in my incessant desire to be noticed. I was extremely immature, even for a seventh grader and if being thirteen wasn't already bad enough two aspects of my character began to emerge during this time that no one seemed to be aware of, not even me, though now I fully recognize them and still have to deal occasionally with the second of those issues.

First of all, I was just plain boy crazy. I thought that if I had a boyfriend my life would be better and I did actually manage to get a boyfriend by spring; a very nice, though somewhat shy, boy named Toby. I can't even begin to comprehend what either one of our parents were thinking but Toby and I went on exactly two dates, driven and picked up by his mother, before I managed to alienate him and Gavin, his best friend, in a way that only I could manage to do.

The three of us, Toby, Gavin and myself, had been invited to a birthday party for a classmate; a backyard cookout. After dinner we were all playing in the backyard when Gavin informed me that he could suddenly grab me from behind and I would not be able to get away. I took this as a serious challenge so of course, I told him to go right ahead and try it. As he grabbed me, I stiffened both of my arms, whirled around as fast as I could and knocked Gavin to the ground. He was actually breathless either from the blow, the fall, or both and actually began to moan about how I had hurt him!

Then, to my complete astonishment, everyone else at the party got mad at me for hurting Gavin! I should mention that Gavin was considered to be an extra cute guy so you can probably guess what that did for any social status I might have gained to that point. At least I hadn't hit my boyfriend that time and I believe that as a result of that incident I at least finally figured out that hitting people wasn't the best way to build relationships or gain popularity, though I was now right back at square one – still in serious need of a boyfriend.

The other, even more destructive element of my character, and the one I still occasionally have to put in its place, was the emergence of a spirit of covetousness and greed. The high school that I attended included in its district several exclusive neighborhoods in north Oklahoma City. (My neighborhood was most definitely not one of them.) Students from these privileged homes were brought daily to school in a long procession of Cadillacs, Lincoln Continentals and an array of expensive sports cars. In fact many of the older students had expensive cars of their own!

My mother drove an ugly green 1954 Ford until it practically fell apart in the street, after that it was a tiny, very basic Corvair for another ten years and then a Plymouth Fury that we called the boat because it was so big; she must have driven that car for about fourteen years (then she gave it to Rhonnie and he drove it for another year or two before he gave it away). As I may have mentioned my mother was very frugal, partly out of fear and partly out of necessity. In writing these words I suddenly realized that I've driven the same car for nine years and my husband now drives the last car my mother ever had, a 1984 Volvo, and it's over twenty years old! I wonder if that tendency could be genetic, at least on my part.

Anyway, all the girls that emerged from these extraordinary cars were absolutely darling. They seemed to have everything imaginable, looks, popularity, and personality and they always seemed to roam in packs. They appeared to have perfect lives, I wanted to be just like them and I wanted everything they had. It wasn't until I was much older that I realized many of these girls that I so idolized weren't necessarily nice people. At least not back then, and truthfully, I doubt they even knew I existed. I hated my life and I both hated and envied them for having lives I wanted. The two things that made their lives the most enviable were the fact that they all had fathers and happy, involved, 'normal' moms; most even had brothers and sisters.

I just knew these girls all lived *Father Knows Best* lives to be sure. I became convinced that if my father hadn't died I would also have endless closets of clothes, shoes, purses and gadgets; not to mention a younger sister to play with or a protective older brother. My life would then be complete, I would be happy, I would belong and most of all I wouldn't be different, awkward or lonely! I was quite relieved when the seventh grade year was over – at least for the summer I wouldn't have to face those girls or my own growing inadequacies.

Aunt Thyra had been the one member of the family who had kept in touch, albeit sporadically, with my Uncle Joe's two children, my cousins Bob and Katie. Bob actually had four children and the oldest was a girl just a year or two younger than I. I was beyond excited when Aunt Thyra brought this cousin, my first cousin once removed to be exact, with her to Oklahoma City for a weekend visit. Though it was our first meeting, we became fast friends and for the next few years we each spent an entire week at first one house, then another. These visits were highly anticipated events for both of us.

It was during one of my earliest visits to my new found cousin's home in Tulsa that I was able to meet my first cousin Katie and her family. I loved everything about Katie at first meeting; her home, her husband, her children, her style, and even though I'm not sure when I had determined that I didn't want to grow up to be like my mother, when I met my cousin Katie I knew I wanted to grow up to be like her. I saw in her family the closest thing to *Father Knows Best* that I had ever seen and her home and family were real. I now had a genuine role model, not just a television show to model my own life after. Though I didn't see Katie again for at least ten years I knew from that moment that she would be a very important influence in my life. Her home is still so charming and I still think that she is one of the most wonderful people I've ever met and in many ways her example served as a beacon to me in later years when my own reality was so dark and dismal.

Then in the middle of my eighth grade year my world turned completely upside down. During that year two boys, two of the funniest and most spontaneous individuals I'd met, sat next to me in my English class. (Our three youngest grandchildren love *Tom and Jerry* cartoons and since I've seen and heard quite a lot of *Tom and Jerry* lately that is what I will call these two.) Tom and Jerry brought out an aspect of my personality, a sense of humor, that had not had the opportunity to develop before and I liked it. They were both absolute comedians and they made me laugh. I love to laugh and these two had been friends since grade school so they were very comfortable with each other and wonder of wonders, they both seemed to really like me. Imagine that! I'd like to think I have a pretty good sense of humor too, but there are just some people who are better at bringing out that facet of my personality than others. If you can make me laugh, I'll just have to confess that I'll be hooked. If I can make you laugh in turn, so much the better! (My husband has that effect on me – we speak our own language, sharing made up words and private jokes as we laugh over things that others wouldn't even begin to understand.)

The more I got to know Tom and Jerry the more I liked them both. The three of us really could have had a nice friendship but my number one goal in life was to have a boyfriend and remember, I also had a knack for really messing things up and soon this became another of those awkward situations that I was so good at getting myself into. Early on I'd begun to develop a really huge crush on Tom and I was absolutely giddy with delight when I realized he seemed to have a crush on me as well. The problem was that both Tom and Jerry wanted to be more than just my friend and that was only the beginning of what turned out to be at least a three year long nightmare.

After a little in-class note writing back and forth, it was established that Tom would be my boyfriend and Jerry and I would be best friends. The most ridiculous part of it all was that I actually thought for awhile that I had found my one true love and the person I would one day marry and with whom I'd have children. In my fantasy world I actually had our children named, three of them, if I recall (and no, there names were not Betty, Bud and Kathy after the Anderson children from *Father Knows Best*). I was, in so far as it is possible for a fourteen year old to be, head-over-heels in love with Tom. I had lost any sense of reason, if in fact I'd ever possessed any, and I was plunging headfirst into a relationship that was soon going to be way over my head. Adolescent hormones and emotions can create a toxic combination, especially if both are left to develop on their own as they had been in my case.

Over the next year Tom and I were a little on again, off again but by my fifteenth birthday we were going steady. It is important for me to stop right there to say that the two of us, thankfully, were never completely alone during the months that this relationship was at its most intense; a very, very good thing and surely strong evidence of God's protection as He scrutinized my path toward what would otherwise have been complete self destruction. I firmly believe that it is only by His grace and mercy that I was able to retain any self respect at all through that relationship. There is little doubt in my mind that if Tom and I had been given even the slightest opportunity we would have had a sexual relationship and neither of us was prepared to even remotely handle that. Still, I was blissfully immersed in this relationship, I didn't have a care in the world or even the slightest thought that I might be heading for disaster. The two of us were officially an item; we were talking on the phone every night and walking the halls before and after school. I had a boyfriend and life was good – for about three months.

I was absolutely blindsided and completely devastated when the relationship abruptly ended for no apparent reason; oh, I was given a reason, it was just one of those explanations that didn't make sense to me. It was something like "It's not you, it's me", or its 60's equivalent, anyway, for more years than I like to remember I was deeply hurt by this sudden rejection. Truthfully, I went just a little crazy in my devastation because the very next day Jerry began calling, at first to offer comfort and support but before long he was making it very clear that he was more than willing to step in and take Toms place as my boyfriend and I let him do so, only to tell him after a very short time - I think it was the next day - that I didn't feel I could be his girlfriend after all.

Now Jerry was the one hurt and I had not only lost my boyfriend, I'd also lost what might have in time become a very nice friend had I not mishandled both relationships from the start. By the spring of my freshman year about all I could do was cry. How I managed to make any passing grades at all that last semester is truly a mystery because I don't remember opening a textbook at all those last few weeks of school. Life at home was getting worse too as my mother and I argued more and more frequently over just about everything; grades, how much freedom I should have and my blatant disrespect and disobedience in general. Except for ballet lessons nothing was right in my world.

After the very painful breakup with Tom and the difficult upheaval of my friendship with Jerry I have to admit that I acted downright shamefully. In the 60's it just was not considered proper for girls to call boys but I called both Tom and Jerry, as well as other friends of theirs often. To put it directly, I pestered the living daylights out of Tom. I would either try to find out where he was and what he was doing from his friends so I could show up there myself or I would have other girls do it for me thinking that would be a little more subtle. I rather imagine that Tom may have felt like he was being stalked and I guess that he was to a certain extent. At one point I even begged Tom to reconcile our relationship because I just couldn't believe that I could have given myself so freely to someone who now wanted nothing to do with me. My emotions were so raw and I felt a level of insecurity as a result of the breakup that I had never experienced before and in addition to that I was humiliated, not only by the breakup but by my own out-of-control behavior; I certainly did not know how to give up gracefully.

It still embarrasses me to think about my high school years - I would really rather not even acknowledge that I went through all that, let alone write about it, except for a couple of things. I'd never had a lot of self esteem, one of my life's recurring themes, and now because of those lost relationships the way I responded to others would be altered for a very long time. I had trusted far too easily but after the humiliation I had just endured I no longer took people at face value and most of all I was determined that no one was ever going to hurt me again.

I was also very aware of the fact that I had reacted horribly yet I didn't seem to know how to change my behavior. I feared that I would conduct myself in the same undignified manner the next time a relationship ended badly. I began to unconsciously keep most individuals at arms length, at least emotionally, oh I dated and even managed to have a few casual friends but I also learned to thoroughly burn my bridges. Keeping others at arms length and writing them off when I was finished with them, or when I thought they might be on the verge of being through with me was the best way I could protect myself.

The second reason I feel compelled to include this, and the next few chapters, in my story is because I now realize that through my particular circumstances I may have been slightly more vulnerable than a lot of teenage girls during the 60's. I was fourteen years old when I began to embark upon a relationship that, though destructive, could have been even more so if I had lived in today's world. As a parent, as well as one who was involved in youth ministry at our church for several years, I know there is much more opportunity for young people to enter into potentially devastating and destructive relationships and behaviors today. Furthermore, the possibilities for devastating consequences today go far beyond what anyone could have imagined in the 60's.

During my high school days teens were not typically left home alone day after day while parents worked; unlike in today's society where most teenagers have way too much unsupervised and idol time on their hands. Drug abuse was seen as something done only by criminals and we had not yet imagined anything like the AIDS epidemic during my teen years. Throw in the potential for unsavory and illicit activity that the internet affords and I can say in all honesty that I am very thankful I am not a teenager today. I can't imagine where I might have ended up given my circumstances and my low self-esteem if I were growing up in today's world.

Even though my mother was very strict, without realizing it, she had inadvertently set me up for the inevitable pain and embarrassment I experienced as a result of too much intimacy by giving me too much freedom long before I was ready to handle it. My mother was normally overly cautious, usually when it was unwarranted and she certainly didn't allow me do everything I wanted to do, in fact, the opposite was true, but on the other hand, as I mentioned before, we never talked to each other about the important things. Our limited discussions about sex always ended with an admonition that sex outside of marriage was just unthinkable; period. Of course that's God's standard, but that was never part of the dialogue, and she never talked to me about emotions or what kind of temptations I might face, and then, how I might deal with those temptations. My mother never dated as a teenager so she was really unable to give me any practical advice or share her experiences with me. Perhaps this was another way she lived vicariously through me. Due to her own lack of experience, as well as her lack of involvement with other parents, she had no comprehension of the potential dangers or that I was too young and too vulnerable for dating.

It surely didn't help that around this same time my grandmother fell and broke her hip, then, a short time later suffered a mild stroke. Sadly, communication between my grandmother and I had begun to wane about the time my mother had allowed me to start dating. I have to wonder if this lack of communication between us was, at least in part, due to the fact that she disapproved of what my mother was allowing and I'm sure she could see that I was becoming more and more out of control.

At any rate there was a lot more tension in our home now and since Granny had always done the cooking and housecleaning my mother had to add those things to her list of responsibilities, which meant of course, that those duties were almost immediately passed on to me. My grandmother's illness weighed heavily upon my mother and she became angrier and more withdrawn than I had ever seen her. My mother and I never worked together to accomplish the things that needed to be done around the house and I never received any gentle guidance from her regarding the practical things; like doing laundry or keeping house. She handled my grandmother's illness and the household responsibilities exactly the same way she had handled my social life when I first began to date; with a list of 'do's' and 'don'ts' and let me tell you, a list of 'do's' and 'don'ts' doesn't begin to adequately equip a teenager for dating or for life.

As a result of my experiences it shouldn't be a big surprise that I'm not a fan of dating as it is often done in our society and I absolutely do not recommend it for anyone as young as I was, no matter how mature they might seem. Remember, I went on my first date when I was in the seventh grade, I believe I had just turned thirteen; the very idea of that horrifies me more than just a little bit. At fourteen, when Tom and I began our dating relationship, I was allowed to 'double date' because Tom had friends that were old enough to drive and even though I was forbidden to go to a drive-in movie with a boy that is exactly where our dates always ended up. Let me just say that other couples in the car don't serve as adequate deterrents to anything!

Amazingly, my mother rarely questioned me about where I went and what I did on my dates. When she did question me I always had a ready lie that would supply her with just the right information and if I were ever late getting home the lie would always keep any trouble to a minimum. She always seemed to believe me, mostly because I think she desperately wanted to; is it possible she just couldn't bear the thought that her child might be untrustworthy? The truth would have sickened my mother had she known the nature of the relationship I'd already been involved in; a relationship that was most certainly out of God's will!

I began this chapter with these verses; "You scrutinize my path and my lying down, and are intimately acquainted with all my ways. Even before there is a word on my tongue, behold, O LORD, You know it all." (Psalm 139: 3-4). Once again, I would say that this knowledge, especially as it pertains to these years of my life might cause me embarrassment and grief but instead I know that they serve as further proof to me of my Fathers steadfast love. In spite of what He saw He already knew how He would one day lead me from that self destructive path I had determined for myself and set my feet upon the one He had planned for me. He chose to be intimately acquainted with all my ways though He found the watching painful. He loved me, He watched me and even when my thoughts, my words and my deeds were so sinful, ugly and destructive He kept His plan and I am so thankful that He knows it all!

Chapter 3
Enclosed

"You have enclosed me behind and before, and laid Your hand upon me. Such knowledge is too wonderful for me; it is too high, I cannot attain to it."
(Psalm 139:5-6)

I began my sophomore year of high school as a complete emotional wreck. The one positive in my life were the ballet classes that I took three to four times a week and I loved them. Ballet was the highlight of my being, the only thing stable and the only part of my life in which I took any real pride. Though my mother paid for only two lessons a week when I was promoted to the more advanced class I was allowed to attend as many extra classes during the week as I wanted. I immersed myself in those classes, dreaming of one day becoming a ballerina and after almost six years of lessons I felt like I was doing very well. One of my most cherished memories is of the day when I was fifteen that my ballet school performed with the Oklahoma City symphony orchestra for area elementary schools. I loved being backstage in the municipal auditorium and the excitement of performing on the large stage; I was sure that day was just the beginning of much greater things to come.

The ballet school I attended was one of the most celebrated in Oklahoma City and every spring The American Ballet Theatre School would visit, to hold auditions for a summer scholarship to attend their school in New York City. I was advanced enough to participate in the auditions when I was fifteen but I don't think the panel of adjudicators even looked at me once. It seems I was the only one on the planet who didn't recognize that I was really not cut out to be a ballerina. Though I was able to do technically all that was required I really was not all that talented and I also was definitely not built like a ballerina.

(The once skinny, awkward child was now a voluptuous, awkward one and ballerinas are just not usually voluptuous, or awkward for that matter.)

At any rate, my dreamed of ballet career came to a screeching halt right after my sixteenth birthday as a result of a knee injury that would take about a year to fully heal. All I have to show for those years are a matching pair of hammer toes; one on each foot (but I will probably always choreograph little ballets in my mind whenever I hear music). When I lost my dream of becoming a ballerina I also lost the will to make anything decent of myself and the downward spiral that I had already begun escalated completely out of control. My life was on a vicious path that would continue for at least ten years, through one marriage and at the expense of two precious children.

My reputation as well as any sense of self worth I might ever have possessed was on its way to ruin long before I injured my knee and I had already begun to attract acquaintances that were soon going to lead me down a path that would be very sinful and unhealthy. I was about to enter a whole new league. Before going any further I'd like to insert a thought from Proverb 17:17; "A friend loves at all times…" It would be many years before I would have a true friend; instead I began to enter into a series of very ungodly alliances. One of my first new 'friends', I'll call her Angela, was a girl whose family had a lot of money, she was beautiful and the kind of person that I felt I would like to be seen with, and best of all she had received a brand new car, a Mustang convertible, on her sixteenth birthday. Angela introduced me to alcohol and cigarettes; both easily accessible because I went to her house almost every day after school and her parents were never at home. It seemed that her parents really didn't care what she did because they scarcely placed any limits on her at all.

Another of the girls in my new circle of alliances, I'll call her Betsy, had a boyfriend that was in his twenties

– we, of course, were only fifteen and sixteen years old. I never really knew for certain just how old he was but he didn't lack friends and I was fixed up on more than one occasion with one or another of them. Betsy lived very, very close to the edge and yet appeared to be very naïve when it served her purpose. She actually had my mother wrapped around her little finger. If my mother had known a fraction of what this girl was really like she would never have ever let me get in the car with her, let alone spend the night with her and on several occasions, no less. Again I must mention that my mother was not always the best judge of character. One thing that I am now aware of as I remember these relationships and the numerous situations I encountered through them is that I don't believe that my mother ever met either of these girls' parents. Now, I don't claim to be an authority on raising teenagers but I think that meeting parents is a fairly basic first step in deciding whether or not your teenagers should be spending a night in their home.

On at least two of those overnight occasions Betsy's boyfriend and one of his friends took us to several nightclubs, one after another, without any regard for the fact that we were so young and though we both looked older I can't imagine now that we looked even remotely old enough to actually be there! At first I was terrified of being caught because if I had been I was sure I would never be allowed to leave the house again, if in fact the world didn't come to an end on the spot. However, after the first few minutes and with the help of a couple of drinks being there became second nature to me. I liked partying and drinking and forgetting that I was a misfit, at least for awhile, not realizing that I was becoming an even greater misfit than I had ever perceived myself to be.

Strangely, though Betsy's boyfriend was very good looking, there was something about his friends that I found disturbingly unattractive and miraculously I managed to get through those dates without so much as a goodnight kiss, in spite of the fact that I was probably quite drunk and therefore very vulnerable. There is no doubt in my mind that was due, once again, to the Lord's hand of protection because I know that Betsy and her boyfriend were sexually active and I'm quite certain in looking back that his friends might have expected no less from me. On those occasions invisibility was a very good thing!

The hedge of protection that God places around His children is truly impermeable and if situations and circumstances call for more than an enclosure He takes us completely out of harms way. "For in the time of trouble He shall hide me in His pavilion: in the secret of His tabernacle shall He hide me; He shall set me up upon a rock." (Psalm 27:5) KJV. If I was invisible in those instances it is surely because the Lord was hiding me in His pavilion and yet I still didn't have a clue. Mercifully, this ungodly alliance came to a sudden end over a misunderstanding that I never did fully comprehend. Distrust and misunderstandings are often the nature of relationships when the Lord is not at the center.

Then there was Peggy, a girl who was at least a year older than I was who also had a boyfriend in his twenties and he was in jail. I don't recall why he was in jail (I am sure though, that whatever the reason it was certainly not his fault). One afternoon Peggy and I went to this jailed boyfriends apartment to get a few things for him. Peggy searched frantically through every drawer in the place. I didn't know what she was looking for and she didn't seem to want my help in looking but I did take notice when she took syringes and a paper bag out of one of the drawers and put them in her purse. My face must have registered some kind of concern because Peggy quickly explained that her boyfriend was diabetic and needed his medication (that was a new one on me but in my naïveté I certainly believed her). I think if I had questioned her I wouldn't have been able to handle or possibly even to comprehend the truth.

If that wasn't bad enough, we proceeded to go from the apartment straight to the jail where we were somehow going to get in to see the boyfriend and deliver his medication to him - sounds almost funny, doesn't it? It was getting dark by the time we arrived there and for me just being on the same block as the jail was frightening enough but Peggy insisted that I accompany her inside. I stood by in embarrassment and humiliation while Peggy made up a story about needing to see her 'brother'. It was now clear to me that something very bad was going on and I was terrified, lying to my mother had become something of an art form, but this kind of thing was truly beyond my comprehension.

Of course, the person with whom Peggy was pleading would not let her see her 'brother' and at that point even though she turned on an incredible amount of charm she could not persuade this man otherwise. As we turned to leave the building Peggy noticed a bank of elevators just around the corner from the reception area and about that time one of the elevators opened. I stood in horrified disbelief as she attempted to step into the elevator only to be intercepted by the man she had just been pleading with a moment earlier. We were firmly escorted from the building, I felt like a criminal and I believe we were mercifully spared what might have been the direst of consequences. I may have even cried at that point which probably was the kiss of death as far as that relationship was concerned. At least as this alliance dissolved I wasn't hurt or confused, just very, very relieved. The rest of that evening is a blur but I'm certain I went home that night feeling like I had scraped the bottom of the barrel but in sad reality my barrel scraping had only just begun.

My next associate, Candace, didn't have money, a car, or a boyfriend, at least not a boyfriend in jail and at first she seemed to really care about me. I was growing increasingly rebellious, my mother and I were not getting along at all now and soon Candace began to encourage my rebellion. Even worse, I would often complain to Candace's mother, Elaine, about my own mother and Elaine was always sympathetic and seemed to encourage my rebellion as well. Elaine readily agreed with me when I told her that my mother was unfair and unreasonable. Candace didn't have a curfew, was allowed to smoke in the house and in fact she and her mother smoked together and I smoked with them. What a disturbing picture that brings to mind. That relationship fell apart when I ran away from home and ended up at their house with Elaine's blessing, of course. When my mother found me later that evening I was grounded for a month, among other things, and forbidden to have any further contact with those two.

Except for one other boyfriend, who I will call Wesley, and an occasional friend, a very nice girl I'll call Liz, the remainder of my high school experience was punctuated by one unsavory relationship after another. I had a string of casual boyfriends, another acquaintance who taught me to shoplift, something I was too terrified to really make a habit of, and my grades remained marginal at best.

What saddens me most is that no one ever once took enough interest in me to take me aside and say to me "You're going the wrong way", "You're making bad choices" or "Did you know Jesus loved you enough that He gave His life for you?" I never once had a Sunday school teacher, Youth Pastor, Christian school teacher or even a Christian peer ask me if I needed someone to talk to or a shoulder to cry on. No one ever offered to share the Lord with me; I'm not sure I would have listened but it might have made a difference if someone had noticed my struggling and taken a genuine interest in me.

On the positive side of things, I did, out of necessity, learn to cook; something that my mother and I would one day laugh about because she never learned to cook anything but a pot roast and for some reason she could make a really good pot roast. I actually liked cooking for my mother and grandmother and I was allowed the latitude to experiment from time to time. Oddly, doing the cooking caused me to remember that in the midst of all the rebellion and turmoil I still had within me an ideal of something that I wanted more than anything in the world. I would often retreat into a fantasy world during dinner preparation and cleanup time as I envisioned my *Father Knows Best* wholesome family though my current path certainly wasn't leading in that direction.

In fact, in writing these words it strikes me how profoundly true that statement is - my Heavenly Father does indeed know best in every situation, all the time and He wants nothing but the very best for His children. How I praise Him and thank Him for His omniscience and for how, even when I didn't know Him, He knew what was best for me and was preparing that for me even though it would be a very long time before I realized His sovereign hand upon my life. It will never cease to amaze me that in the midst of my rebellion He upheld and preserved me. He understood my thought from afar and He understood how important that thought, my precious childhood dream, was to me and how one day that dream would fit perfectly with the plan He already had for my life. Oh, how I praise Him!

As for Wesley, I met him towards the end of my sophomore year through a young family for whom I regularly babysat. This family lived in our neighborhood and for some reason they really seemed to like me and they trusted me with their precious little girl and because of that trust I believe I was a different person when I was with them. Wesley, who was four years older than I, was in college when we met, he was from another town so he knew absolutely nothing about me or my reputation and when he asked me out I was beyond flattered. I saw in him an opportunity, at least at first, to make some needed changes and to do things a little differently. Wesley was a genuinely nice young man and I cared for him a great deal but in looking back on our relationship I think he may not have known quite what to make of me. Our dating relationship was also a little on again, off again for a variety of reasons, not the least of which was distance. It was also a very confusing relationship, at least for me.

Wesley was goal-oriented, responsible and focused; character traits that both drew me and angered me at the same time. When things were going well between us I actually had a desire to do better in school. I knew that Wesley had very definite goals, he came from a large, close-knit family (definitely *Father Knows Best* material) and there was also the fact that he was in college; a definite status symbol, even if no one else was impressed. I realized early on in our relationship that I would need to have some definite goals myself and become much more responsible if he was ever going to become truly serious about me. Eventually though, I succeeded in bringing Wesley down to my standards instead. "Bad company corrupts good morals." (1 Corinthians 15:33-34).

After a very short time our dating fell into a familiar destructive pattern yet I managed, again miraculously, to still retain my virginity. I often felt that I was being used by Wesley but by the same token I believe that he may have felt that I was using him. Though we were somewhat physically involved I succeeded in protecting my emotions, though just barely, because every time it seemed that he was truly interested in me he would back away and I would get hurt and angry. Of course, I realize now that he must have known that I was not right for him and I also realize that my feelings for him were not as deep, or as pure, as I pretended they were. Going our separate ways was probably a very good thing except once again I was never quite sure when or how that decision was made.

Wesley had arranged to spend the summer of 1965 doing something that sounded really exciting to me. He was going to be a forest ranger, or something that seemed equally as interesting in another state. This posed a problem for me because even though Wesley and I only dated occasionally I had hoped that we would be able to date during the summer. I was also a little bothered by his plan because years earlier, when my family had visited Carlsbad Caverns, I had so loved the experience of being in the desert, watching the bats fly out of the cave at twilight and just generally thinking that I might like to be a forest ranger myself someday, if my plans to become a ballerina didn't materialize. Wesley had never expressed any such interest to me and I had never told him of my interest either but I was a little angry (I was really just plain jealous) that he would be having the opportunity to do something that I think I would have enjoyed doing very, very much and I wasn't looking forward to spending another summer alone.

One other thing I should mention about Wesley is that he didn't drink at all and even though I didn't drink when I was with him by the end of my junior year in high school I was drinking every chance I could. It truly amazes me that a high school girl could have alcohol so readily available to her in the 60's and again, the situation is far worse for young people today. My drinking opportunities would have come even more often had I not been grounded for one reason or another a lot of the time. I was in a perpetual state of punishment and the arguments at home had escalated to the point that I actually hit my mother with a hairbrush once and in return she slapped me so hard that I fell backwards onto the bed. I'm not sure how long I was grounded after that incident.

More often than not though, the punishments were a consequence of my attitude; I very rarely got into trouble for something I had done because I was rarely caught in wrongdoing. Sadly, on the rare occasion I was caught doing something wrong, the only thing punishment accomplished was that I learned to do wrong just a little better, to be a little sneakier and get by just a little longer between punishments. The one thing I never learned was how to avoid incurring my mother's inevitable wrath over the little things because I just couldn't manage to keep from being on the offensive when I did get into trouble. In short, my mouth got me into far more trouble than my actions.

My mother continued to be both too strict and far too lenient at the same time. She wouldn't let me get my ears pierced because she didn't like the way that looked but she never met me face to face at the door when I came home from an evening out. She always knew when I came in because she was quick to reprimand if I was even a minute late so I learned that I could come home in any condition I wanted to as long as I got home on time.

Only once did she ever question me about the smell of alcohol and I explained to her that someone else had been drinking and had spilled it on me. I was both appropriately disgusted over the incident and indignant that she would suggest I'd been drinking. If I remember correctly she questioned me about this in the dark otherwise she would have realized that I was most surely lying and in fact had had quite a bit to drink.

I believe my mother did the very best she knew how to do and I know she loved me with all her heart even though I'm sure I made her feel like giving up many times. I think she had simply reached a point where she just didn't know what to do with me and I certainly wasn't making her job any easier (I do thank God every day that none of my children were as difficult to raise as I was). She didn't have a clue as to how to go about getting any help in dealing with me either and had turned her back on her best source of help when she'd turned her back on the Lord a few years earlier.

My junior year English class had been particularly difficult and I had struggled to maintain a C average in that class most of the year. Part of the problem truly was the teacher, a bubbly young woman who had likely not been out of school very long herself. She probably was a very fine teacher as long as those she was teaching caught on quickly and required a minimum of help. I fit into neither category; she might as well have been trying to teach English concepts to me in Swahili. Much of what this teacher presented went way over my head and my questions seemed to frustrate her. Her answers to my questions certainly frustrated me so I very quickly stopped asking them and I began to get lost very early on in that class. I was completely lost by the fourth quarter of that year; I was failing eleventh grade English and the teacher didn't seem to care. There were far too many bright and promising students in class for her to bother with someone who wasn't going to get it anyway. Surely I was as invisible as I have ever been in that classroom because it was certainly evident to me that I was going to fail and I can't imagine that it was any less evident to the teacher but I don't recall any effort being made on her part to prevent that certainty. My grade for the final semester of that horrific class was just as expected; a solid F.

My high school handled the distribution of year end grades by mailing them to the students, usually about a week after school was out for the summer. Since my mother worked every day I almost always got the mail so it was easy for me to intercept my grades when they arrived. When the report card arrived it contained no surprises, the usual C's, maybe one B and the F in English. The report had been created on a typewriter and the paper was such that with the careful use of a lead pencil I was able to artfully and skillfully turn that F into a B, which actually raised my English grade for the year from its previous C to yet another B, again by the artful and skillful use of the pencil. Imagine that, my mother would be so proud of me! I was certainly quite proud of myself and I would have all summer to figure out how I would explain having to retake the class in the fall. I was only slightly concerned about what the consequences might be if my mother ever found out I'd altered my grade because I didn't think that she would find out and sure enough, she did not. I didn't know then that soon we would all have a lot more to worry about and even the F in English would pale in comparison to what was soon to come!

On the last day of my junior year in high school Wesley had planned to be in Oklahoma City for part of the day and I was under the impression that we would at least be able to spend part of the afternoon together before he went to his home, about fifty miles away, for a day or two before he would begin his ranger duties. That day I also had an appointment for a routine visit with my doctor; probably a follow up on the knee injury. I begged my mother to reschedule that appointment because I didn't want to miss my opportunity to say goodbye to Wesley but she wouldn't hear of it so I went to the appointment thinking that if we were able to get in and out of the clinic quickly I would still have time to at least see Wesley for a few minutes before his departure.

All the members of our household had gone to the same physician, Dr. Stan Kyle, since the day we arrived in Oklahoma City and we all liked him and because we had all been his patients for several years he seemed to know us really well. Dr. Kyle seemed to always have time to sit and chat, cared about how we were doing and when the visit was over you never felt as if you'd been rushed; an attribute that we all liked on most days. However, none of us knew on this particular day that Dr Kyle had aspirations to leave Family Practice and move to the field of Psychiatry and was, in fact, actively working toward that goal.

I know that I was visibly anxious when we arrived for the appointment and I was growing more and more distressed when, first the wait, and then the visit, seemed to be taking longer than usual. I just wanted to leave, maybe I could still be home in time to see Wesley, but instead, Dr. Kyle asked my mother to leave the room and then began to question me about school, boys, my home life, etc. I could no more have articulated my feelings at that point because the anger I'd felt toward my mother for not rescheduling this appointment now became directed at sweet Dr. Kyle. I don't remember what I told him that day, and I don't know what he said to my mother on the other side of the examining room door, all I know is that we were gone from the house, and more important, the telephone for much longer than we should have been. The ride home took forever and that time was magnified by the extreme silence between my mother and me on the way home.

I already knew my most immediate problem that summer would be loneliness like I had never experienced before because the kind of acquaintances I'd been drawing the last couple of years were not the kind with whom I'd been able to build lasting, quality relationships. The only person who I thought I might be able to count on would be gone the entire summer. I'd finally given up on Tom after learning that he had become very seriously involved with one of the rich (and beautiful) girls that I still watched with envy. My summer job that year would be babysitting for the two year old girl that lived across the street and though she was darling and I loved her family very much, she was, after all, two years old. I really wanted just one best friend and a nice, reliable boyfriend, but the nice people that might have been my friends under other circumstances, like Liz, no longer wanted anything to do with me. We had not been home from the doctors' visit very long when the telephone rang; I ran to answer hoping it would be Wesley on the other end of the line.

My heart sank as the person on the other end of the line began to introduce himself as Carl, whom I had never met but knew that we'd been in the same study hall during the past year. I thought I was having a great deal of difficulty hiding my disappointment upon realizing that the caller was not Wesley but Carl didn't seem to notice. In fact I was angry and fighting back tears as Carl continued to talk; if only caller ID had been invented in the early 50's (yes, this was 1965 but my family was always way behind the times when it came to technology). I knew who Carl was and had been told he was interested in me (and not for the most wholesome reasons either, I might add). Even knowing that Carl was questioning others about me I was unprepared for his call and didn't have a ready excuse when he asked me out. I truly would not have answered the phone if I'd known it was Carl because I wasn't even slightly interested in him.

All I knew about Carl was that he was a year older than I was and in fact, had just graduated. We had exactly one mutual acquaintance; a boy neither of us knew very well but who had also been in our study hall and had attended the same church I attended with my grandmother. I hung up the phone that day perplexed that I had agreed to date someone that I really didn't want to date but rationalized it all with the expectation that we would go out exactly once or twice and that would be the end of it. If I found that I really didn't want to continue to date him I would display my disinterest then he would lose interest in me; at least that was my thought. Instead, I was about to enter into the most ungodly relationship that I had entered into yet, a relationship that would very nearly destroy me and would very nearly destroy Carl as well.

Within the week Carl and I had our first date and quite honestly it was dreadful and uncomfortable, at least until we got to our destination; a drive-in movie, what else? As soon as the car was parked Carl proceeded to unpack a gallon container of a concoction of grain alcohol and grape juice, something he called 'purple passion'. I had no problem drinking beer, I actually liked beer, I was accustomed to drinking it by now and I knew how much beer I could drink before I became affected by it (not that I always stopped at that point). But I had no idea how much more potent this stuff was going to be and even though I should have planned to keep my wits about me this evening I dove blindly in. I figured it would help make the evening more bearable and to make matters even worse I was starting to feel a little sorry for Carl, though right now I couldn't begin to tell you why. I was totally unprepared for the effect that this drink would have on me; I was probably drunk within fifteen minutes and I found I simply did not care. As soon as Carl realized the state I was in he was all over me and I only feebly resisted. Life as I had wanted it to be didn't matter to me anymore and worse, my gut feeling told me that Carl was not going to go away any time soon, no matter what I might do to discourage him.

How I wish I had done so many things differently over the next few months. Carl began calling at least once a day, showing up on our doorstep unannounced and my mother, whose judgment of character was fifty-fifty at best, actually liked him, at least in the beginning! Absolutely no one else, girl or boy, was calling me at all that summer and even though I felt more and more violated, at least emotionally, every time I was with Carl he seemed to become more and more confident in the relationship and I gradually became more and more resigned to it. I believe that in his way he really cared for me, he certainly told me often enough that he loved me as he repeatedly tried to convince me that I cared for him and he'd certainly managed to convince himself that I did. One thing was certain, he was very attentive but I didn't recognize all this attention as being potentially possessive and the best part of this relationship is that I didn't have to work at it like I'd had to work to maintain my relationships with Tom and Wesley. I dated Carl but still dreamed of the one who would one day be my *Father Knows Best* perfect husband because it surely wasn't going to be him.

Before I delve any further into this episode in my life I want to emphasize that Carl was not really a bad person, although we definitely started our relationship on the wrong foot. Carl was just plainly and simply very, very bad for me and in all fairness and honesty I was equally bad for him. We certainly didn't bring out the best in each other. We didn't even make each other laugh, in fact over the next few years just the opposite would be true as my extensive collection of tears would be added to considerably and on numerous occasions. The wonderful, godly man that has been my pastor since 1982 once said that one should never even date a person they wouldn't want to marry. Truer words have probably never been spoken. Oh, how I wish I'd heard them back then and after having heard would have been wise enough to take those words to heart!

Except for the time spent with Carl, the summer of 1965 went by entirely too quickly and the excitement of being a senior was lost to me when I returned to school in the fall. For one thing, I had the English class problem looming over my head; I had managed to talk my school counselor into allowing me to enroll in both the junior and senior English classes assuring her that if I had a different teacher for junior English that I would be able to pass both classes but quite honestly I wasn't sure about that at all. I also had to explain to my mother why I was taking two English classes and I dealt with that problem by telling her I had been selected to take some kind of experimental class for extra credit or something equally as lame and, as usual, she didn't question me.

The problem that concerned me more was that even though Carl, my now official 'boyfriend' had graduated the year before there were several people at school who knew him and apparently he wasn't well thought of by everyone. He would pick me up at school frequently, I was being seen with him far more than I wanted to be and I soon found out that he had done quite a lot of talking over the summer about the fact that we were an item. Why anyone would have bragged about that back then I'll truly never know. (Oh, and I found out a few years later that during this time my old friend Jerry told Carl that he and I had been sexually intimate and I was never able to convince Carl that this was a bald-faced lie.)

  The bottom line is that my reputation was now completely ruined. My mother was starting to dislike Carl and even though I wanted out of the relationship myself, she was unknowingly pushing me towards him by continually making her feelings about him known. If I've learned anything through the years it is that parents have a responsibility to express their concerns but I'm not sure how productive it is when even the simplest conversation ends in an attempt to drive a point home. Now I was trying to keep conversation with my mother to a minimum but I now also recognize that part of her concern was likely due to my own lack of enthusiasm for the relationship that she surely had to be sensing.

  All the challenges my mother encountered as a widowed parent and all the issues I faced as a fatherless child could have been dealt with so much better if our household had taken heed of Psalm 68:5-6. "A father of the fatherless and a judge for the widows is God in His holy habitation. God makes a home for the lonely; He leads out the prisoners into prosperity, only the rebellious dwell in a parched land." How I wish my mother had known that God was for her and not against her (Romans 8:31). And though I refuse to dwell on regrets of the past I do wish I had realized that my Heavenly Father was there for me during those rebellious years as well. During those times when I thought to myself, "If my father were here I wouldn't behave this way" I didn't know that I had a Heavenly Father who was just as present and more than able to provide for my every need. Instead of looking to the Lord for help my mother had chosen to live in anger and bitterness and I willfully chose to dwell in a parched land through my sin of rebellion.

I am absolutely certain of this: our Heavenly Father knows and cares about every detail of the lives of His children. Even when He saw my disobedience and rebellion accelerating, when He saw my determination to do things my own way (though I knew that what I was doing was wrong) even then, He continued to love me in a way that only He could. Even at the very height of my rebellion "(He had) enclosed me behind and before, and laid (His) hand upon me." (Psalm 139:5). My Father continued to hedge me in even as I tried on so many occasions to get past His hedge of protection and the safety of my mother's authority. I see very clearly that because of my determination to do my own thing, my own way that He finally allowed a circumstance that would direct the course of my life in a way that I surely would not have chosen if I had been listening to Him and seeking His plan and His will. The words of Isaiah 30:1-3 best sum up the end of my childhood in "'Woe to the rebellious children,' declares the LORD, 'Who execute a plan, but not Mine, And make an alliance, but not of My Spirit, In order to add sin to sin; Who proceed down to Egypt without consulting Me, to take refuge in the safety of Pharaoh and to seek shelter in the shadow of Egypt! Therefore the safety of Pharaoh will be your shame and the shelter in the shadow of Egypt, your humiliation.'"

At the beginning of senior year this rebellious child was nearing the end of her rope. I knew I wouldn't be able to keep up with the demands of school, I couldn't stand my mother's now constant harping and I would no longer be able to bear the loneliness I felt as I walked through the halls of my high school day after day all by myself. Carl continued to be assertive and sure of himself (and sure of us as a couple) and I resigned myself to the fact that he was probably going to be the best I could ever do. I was quite certain of one thing; that no one else would ever want me or be able to love me now and sadly, I saw in this relationship, destructive as it was, a way out of my most immediate problems.

Together, Carl and I executed a plan that certainly wasn't of God. We entered into an alliance, but not of His Spirit, His will or His timing, adding sin upon sin. I willingly proceeded into this alliance as surely as if I had walked into the captivity of Egypt. If I had consulted my Father I know that He would have provided me another refuge, a better place of safety but I took refuge in something that was not of Him. Ultimately that deviant plan resulted in my own shame and humiliation. Not to mention the pain it caused numerous others.

The consequences of all that sin and rebellion came to a head early one November morning when after my mother drove me to school, I went straight to my locker, dropped off the school books I was carrying, gathered my personal belongings and walked right back out of that school before the first bell. I never looked back. This ghastly plan of ours amounted to nothing more than an elaborate way for me to run away from home and two weeks later I married someone that I knew I didn't love so I could escape my mother's wrath, the demands of school and even (or maybe especially) my own personal failures. Just as the rebellious children took refuge in the captivity of Egypt I jumped, that beautiful, crisp fall day, from the frying pan into a fire of my own creation and that fire would burn more deeply and destructively than I could ever have imagined!

Chapter 4
At the Edge of the Grave

"Where can I go from Your Spirit? Or where can I flee from Your presence? If I ascend to heaven, You are there; if I make my bed in Sheol, behold, You are there." (Psalm 139:7-8)

When I was four years old my family visited Meteor Crater in Arizona. My mother had likely already recognized my propensity for pushing the limits because she had purchased a leash with a harness contraption that went around my body to insure that I would keep a safe distance from the edge of the crater. I remember that I highly resented this confinement and resisted the leash with all my might; as far as I could tell I was the only one there with a leash which added greatly to my sense of indignation. I remember pulling against it to get as close as I possibly could to the edge; even at four years of age I was proving to be a challenge to my mother and I was beginning a pattern of seeing just how far I could get into something without being consumed by it. I had already begun to live very close to the edge years before Carl entered my life.

There is an old saying, "if you play with fire you're going to get burned" and I'd sat at the edge of my personal frying pan for years, getting as close as I possibly could to the edge without actually falling in to the fire. But the leash was gone now and I had pushed every parental limit imaginable while I toyed with those flames getting closer and closer until I'd lost my balance completely. I was now immersed in flames! Thank God for the wonderful, soothing balm in Gilead; the best burn ointment the world has ever known because I would soon need it.

I often refer to my adolescence as my 'frying pan years' (right before jumping squarely into the fire), and those years had been truly uncomfortable, unpleasant and unhappy but the knowledge that I could have made those years a little better for myself with a better attitude hasn't helped me deal with the memories of them at all. Truly, I feel that before I write another word I should apologize to anyone who may have experienced true horror as a child because I now realize I led a rather sheltered, even somewhat privileged life compared to so many.

I can't begin to comprehend being abused or neglected yet I know so many lovely, godly women who have not just survived, but overcome unfathomable mistreatment. I'm always awed and humbled by their examples of strength, grace and forgiveness and I praise God for His restoration and the healing He has brought to their lives. Through a horror I had created for myself, as well as for those who loved me, I was about to find out just what it meant to be in a truly uncomfortable and unpleasant place. I was barely in mid-leap into that fire when I realized the frying pan hadn't been so bad after all; in fact it was beginning to look quite safe and rather cozy.

My life as a new wife began completely differently than I had envisioned or ever hoped that it would one day. Like every little girl I had dreamed of a long, white wedding gown and veil, a honeymoon in Paris or perhaps a Caribbean cruise, then settling immediately into a neat little cottage with a white picket fence. But for me there had been no romantic proposal on bent knee, no bridal registries, festive showers or engraved invitations. There had been no flowers, color schemes or bridesmaids dresses to choose, just a lot of scheming and a few quick decisions, followed by tearful confessions and angry confrontations leading up to the day of the sober and less-than-elegant ceremony. (I wore the best dress I owned, a dark brown plaid two-piece set that was already fitting a little too snugly.) I felt like anything but a bride.

Instead of offering congratulations or best wishes on my 'wedding' day my mother sent me off by declaring that she would have preferred seeing our names in the obituaries rather than the marriage license column of the newspaper. Ironically, after the first sexual encounter I'd had with Carl, I actually went home thinking that if I became pregnant I would simply kill myself, because as I mentioned, I really didn't think the future held much for me anymore. I had cried all the way through that encounter; something Carl arrogantly mistook for my being overcome with emotion and undying love.

By the time the second month of our relationship had rolled around I didn't have thoughts of suicide anymore but I still might have readily agreed with my mother's sentiment except that my foolish, stubborn pride and rebellious, defiant attitude would not soon allow me to admit any mistakes I'd made. Instead, I harbored a great deal of blame and ill-feeling toward her, I continued to declare that if my father had lived this never would have happened and I stormed out from under my family's umbrella of protection and into my new life.

My mother would remain cool and distant for several weeks and my grandmother and Aunt Thyra were also deeply hurt and disappointed in me so consequently I had a great deal of difficulty facing them as well for a very long time. I was filled with remorse over the direction my life had taken and that there had been absolutely no one at all that I could confide in. Before the ink was even dry on the marriage license problems between Carl and I began to surface. I was completely exhausted, stressed and emotionally drained and quite frankly the wedding night didn't hold any special significance for me. It certainly wasn't something I was looking forward to, I wanted nothing more than to crawl into a hole and be left completely alone as reality very abruptly set in. Instead of that dreamed of romantic getaway I prepared dinner, and then Carl and I went to, of all places, a drive-in movie. How's that for a 'honeymoon'? I didn't even have a wedding ring and perhaps the saddest part of all is that it really didn't matter to me that I didn't have one.

    I spent the first few weeks of marriage trying to figure out an elaborate scheme to completely disappear and I would spend the next nine years trying to figure out just how I had gotten into first, a relationship that I had no desire for and then, a marriage that was smothering me and causing we to feel trapped. My *Father Knows Best* fantasy was replaced by a daydream to board a bus and head for California, of all places, but I didn't have a cent to my name nor did I have even a workable fantasy plan for what I would do when I arrived there. Now that I actually wanted to be invisible all eyes seemed to be disapprovingly on me. Carl had rented the tiniest apartment imaginable; except for a kitchen you could barely turn around in, and the bathroom, there was only one room that served as both living room and bedroom (Murphy bed and all). I think that would be close quarters even for two people who couldn't get enough of each other and I'd had enough before we'd even begun and there was absolutely no place for me to hide.

    When I wasn't dreaming of escape to California I was wishing I could go home to my mother and grandmother to be the family baby again. If only starting completely over had been possible but I was no longer the family baby, I was the black sheep of the family; a transformation that seemed to have occurred virtually overnight. I found that I was not just uncomfortable around my family but because my shame and humiliation was so great I dreaded running into anyone who might know me from school, I even felt a sense of disapproval from total strangers so I rarely left the apartment.

    I continued to believe that my life would have been oh, so different if I'd had a father's love to guide me and to protectively meet my dates at the door. I have only recently come to realize the magnitude of the fact that when

I met Carl I had absolutely no self esteem or sense of self worth left. The 'if onlys' of my childhood and teenage years became the 'if onlys' of my relationship with Carl and our marriage and the next several years to come would be punctuated by lots more 'if onlys'. Though I've said it before I believe it bears repeating; I had been so hurt and I was so lonely and desperate that even though I really didn't want to go out with Carl on even one date I simply lacked the will to say so. Going on that first date and then later giving in had just simply been easier than saying no.

The best advice I could give to anyone in a similar situation is that decisions that are driven by desperation, loneliness or lack of self worth will leave you even more desperate, lonely and with a sense of even less self esteem and you will likely take others down with you when you travel that road. I wanted to blame Carl for being forceful, for preying on my vulnerabilities, even for making that first phone call, but the fact of the matter is that I had placed myself in a position that I should not have been in, very definitely the wrong place at the wrong time (and not just once, but many times over) because I didn't think I deserved to have what I really wanted out of life. I just simply believed that I wasn't pretty enough, I wasn't smart enough, I wasn't desirable enough, lies, yes, but those vicious lies created a truth of their own and that truth was that I didn't think enough of myself to pursue my dreams because in the end, I felt so unworthy of them.

God's word makes a very important statement about who we are and why in Ephesians 2:10. "For we are His workmanship, created in Christ Jesus for good works, which God prepared beforehand so that we would walk in them." Another element of our fearful and wonderful making yet I thought so little of God's workmanship in those days and I had no regard for any good works that He might have prepared for me. How precious is the testimony of the young person who has been taught from a very young age who he or she is in Christ Jesus and has been wise enough to take that teaching to heart. I thought my dreams for a happy family and a solid, moral life were just pipe dreams and that those dreams only came true for a select and privileged few who by fate or happenstance were positioned in the right place at the right time by their life's circumstances. Yet another lie and I believed every word.

It is certainly not my intention to vilify Carl in any way; we were both instrumental in creating the mess we were making of our lives. One of the saddest things that I held against Carl was the fact that like me, he was also different. I was becoming more and more aware of this fact and I was truly beginning to hate him for it. Furthermore, the fact that he didn't seem to notice that he was different or was not bothered by that fact only made matters worse for me. We were both the only children of mothers who were raising us alone, Carl really didn't have a clue about what it took to be a husband or father and my only role model had been a perfect and fictional TV character. There is just no better way to say it, in addition to the fact that both of us were selfish and immature, the way I saw it we were both, fatherless, penniless misfits! Carl did work very hard to provide for us and right before we were married he joined the Air National Guard which helped to supplement his income.

In spite of the fact that it should have been completely obvious to him by now that I really didn't love him he continued to proclaim his love for me, though I now realize that his love was really more of an obsession. (Carl readily admitted that his attraction to me from the beginning had been purely physical and throughout our marriage I believe he continued to see me more as a possession than a partner.) Occasionally I see a T-shirt that bears the slogan *"Doesn't Play Well With Others"*; we both should have worn that T-shirt when we stood before the minister on our wedding day!

From the beginning I knew we had nothing positive in common and our common backgrounds just worked against us. We didn't have similar goals, interest or ideals, we didn't like the same music, movies or television shows. We would never have any real friends in common; we didn't even like the same food and those differences would remain throughout the marriage. Carl didn't like cats all that well either but at least tolerated them off and on, but later in our marriage he would often take his anger toward me out on one of my cats and that didn't set well with me at all. At least I'll say this much; we were not unequally yoked, not spiritually anyway. I would also dare make the statement that our relationship was in direct opposition to God's definition of love. "Love is patient, love is kind and is not jealous; love does not brag and is not arrogant, does not act unbecomingly; it does not seek its own, is not provoked, does not take into account a wrong suffered, does not rejoice in unrighteousness, but rejoices with the truth; bears all things, believes all things, hopes all things, endures all things." (1 Corinthians 13:4-7). Do you have to ask what was lacking in our relationship with one another?

Gradually, over the months that followed the marriage my mother and I did eventually come to better terms; after the initial shock of my becoming pregnant, dropping out of school and marrying Carl my family began to look forward, at least to some extent, to the birth of the coming baby. Looking forward to the birth of the baby was the bright spot in my life too. I devoured every bit of information I could on pregnancy, childbirth and child rearing and practically marked the days until the due date off on the calendar.

I didn't know enough to wonder about where in the world we would put another human being in the tiny apartment (thinking ahead was definitely not one of my strong suits back then) and as it turned out that wouldn't be an issue because two weeks before the baby's birth Carl would be going to Biloxi, Mississippi for a year of active duty with the National Guard. It was decided that when he left for Mississippi I would move out of the apartment and back home with my mother and grandmother until the baby and I could join him. I wasn't sold on the idea of moving to Mississippi but I welcomed the opportunity to be back at home and at least for the days prior to the baby's birth it was a very good move. I felt happier and more relaxed than I had in months.

Ten days after Carl's departure our darling little boy was born and because Carl and I could never agree upon a name he was named him after his father by default. I however, would never be able to call our child by his name and began calling him Andy almost immediately. Andy was simply the cutest thing that I had ever seen and he was certainly the cutest baby in the nursery, perhaps even the universe. (He's grown into a very wonderful, sweet and handsome young man, too!) The birth went like clockwork and I actually enjoyed having my mother close by while I labored. She even bragged about how brave I was and how proud she was of both me and the baby. Was that the first time I'd ever experienced her pride in me? I admit that I was very proud of my accomplishment and I finally felt I'd done something worthwhile and the next few weeks were for the most part very peaceful and as carefree as can be imagined with a newborn in the house.

We had set the date for our move to be about two months after Andy's birth. As the date drew closer my mother once again became sullen and moody. She began to make suggestions, at first subtle ones, that Andy and I would be better off if we didn't go to Mississippi. I would surely have been tempted to stay in Oklahoma City and under her roof but she was also starting to become critical of me and I quickly realized that I would be absolutely miserable if I remained there. In the end she agreed to drive us to Mississippi after she had exhausted all the 'worst case scenarios' she could think of.

On the way there, while she had a captive audience she told me, among other things that Andy, who was the picture of health, would probably die in Mississippi from poverty or neglect. We weren't even out of Oklahoma when I knew the decision to join Carl was the only decision I could possibly have made given the limited options I had before me. My parenting abilities and my poor judgment were discussed again after we had stopped for a bathroom break and I'd changed Andy's diaper in the backseat of the car. My mother, in her usual fearful approach to life, became almost irrational in pointing out that someone might have seen me changing the baby and might even follow us in order to kidnap him. It was just one of many strange and uncomfortable conversations as she seemed to grasp opportunities out of thin air to criticize both my parenting and my judgment or accuse me of neglect. I never neglected the baby – I scarcely let him out of my sight! Oh yes, I was good and ready to get out of the car and move forward as best I could when we finally arrived at our destination!

The year that followed was spent living barely hand to mouth in first, an apartment that was only slightly bigger than the one we'd left behind, then after the first few months to a roomy cottage across the street that had a separate room for little Andy. In retrospect the year was actually quite good for us. There's just nothing like being in a strange place, hundreds of miles from family, or anything else familiar to cause a person to grow up a little bit and stand on his, or her, own two feet. That was something we both needed very, very badly. Life in Mississippi was very difficult though; not only was money extremely tight, Andy and I were left alone for twelve to fifteen hours on many a day. When Carl and I were together we argued frequently and about absolutely everything under the sun. We were steadily seeing more and more things in each other that we didn't like very much and the stress of holding down a part-time job along with his military obligations was beginning to show on Carl. I found myself walking on eggshells a lot and then blowing up when I couldn't tiptoe any longer; much the way I had handled my mother's moodiness.

I did manage to make a few friends in Mississippi among some other young military wives in the same penniless and lonely situation that I was in but the shame and humiliation of the circumstances of my marriage were always at the forefront of my mind. When asked, I would tell my new friends that Carl and I had married a few months earlier than we actually had and I made up incredible stories about an elaborate and beautiful wedding, sharing every detail from my Uncle Joe giving me away to the colors of the bridesmaids' dresses.

When Carl and I married Aunt Thyra had taken a few pictures with a new camera that she was still learning to use. For some reason which always seemed just a little prophetic to me, the pictures, when developed showed nothing but black; as if the lens cap had been left on the camera. There were no pictures to commemorate the day, not that I would have ever showed them to anyone. Instead, I would explain to my new friends that I had left our numerous wedding pictures at my mother's house for safekeeping. I even told people that I had graduated from high school a year early! I'm afraid I would be hard pressed to remember all the intricacies of the tales I told about my circumstances to make me feel a little less ashamed of myself (as well as more like everyone else). I wonder now how many people that actually observed Carl and I together questioned either what had happened to us or how much of what I'd said about us was true.

In spite of the fact that I was unhappy in the marriage I absolutely loved being a mom and I had let it be known right up front that I would stay at home to care for my children. I'd always had strong feelings about being a stay at home mom and this would not be negotiable. I also lacked any marketable skills whatsoever and since I didn't have even a high school diploma I likely wouldn't have been able to find a job that would adequately cover childcare expenses and still leave any worthwhile amount of money.

Despite the fact that we didn't have a car for the first six months I found I actually enjoyed living in Biloxi and the lack of a car didn't seem to be that great a burden. We were within comfortable walking distance of the Air Force Base, Carl's part time job and a small grocery store. Almost daily I would put Andy in his stroller and walk two blocks to the beach, my new favorite place; I loved the fact that even in the winter many a day was warm enough to wear shorts. While my life was certainly not the *Father Knows Best* one I had so idealized as a child I was, at least for a time, able to dig in my heels and make the best of it.

When Carl's year of active duty was completed we decided to move to Tulsa and I was glad that we would not be returning to Oklahoma City to live. It had been very good for me to be somewhere other than the place where I had so many bad memories and I had loved Tulsa as a child. Aunt Thyra lived in an apartment in downtown Tulsa and I had always considered visiting her an adventure and as I explored the downtown area I got to know it and its beautiful historic buildings well. In fact, I felt more comfortable in Tulsa and with Aunt Thyra than I did with my mother because my relationship with my mother remained difficult and unpredictable, just like my relationship with Carl.

Even after a year of living hundreds of miles apart my mother still watched me like a hawk when we were together and she continued to be very critical of even the smallest things. Nevertheless it would be nice having a family member close by and Aunt Thyra doted on my new little one the way she had doted on me as a child. I hoped that things would be better in Tulsa and for a couple of years they were better because Carl immediately got a very nice and secure job with the help of a family friend and money, though we were not exactly rolling in it, was not quite as scarce as it had been the first two years of our marriage.

After settling in Tulsa I saw Aunt Thyra a couple of times a week; she would often take Andy and me out for a day going to lunch and shopping and I was actually enjoying life to an extent. There were still arguments and ups and downs with Carl but they were getting a little more predictable and manageable and we eventually were even able to move into a spacious two bedroom apartment in a nice part of town. I now thought that perhaps things would improve even more if we had another baby. How's that for rational thinking? Maybe *Father Knows Best* wasn't so out of reach after all and within the year of our move to Tulsa I was pregnant again.

Two and a half years after the birth of our son a darling little girl, Jennifer Eileen, was born, six weeks later Carl and I bought a house and I was now busy being as domestic as I could be. I completely settled in to my new found status as mother of two and for a few months all went well as I busied myself with the children and settling into the house.

The house was about thirty years old and needed a great deal of work though; there was no air conditioning, the old carpets and linoleum were in the worst possible condition, every room needed painting and there would be plumbing and electrical issues to deal with on a regular basis. The novelty of the house quickly began to wear off and I became more overwhelmed everyday with the increasing realization that playing house and keeping house, especially that house which seemed to be falling down around us, were two very different things.

My grandmother had been a meticulous housekeeper. My mother, on the other hand, loved books and when she wasn't working she quite simply preferred reading or playing the piano to anything domestic and that is exactly the way she spent her evenings and weekends. Even though I had plenty of opportunity to learn from my grandmother's example I had learned my housekeeping skills from my mother, who by her own admission was probably the world's worst housekeeper. In addition to not really knowing the first thing about running a home I also wanted things to be perfect and they certainly were not perfect so I soon gave up trying. I was amazed at the amount of work it took to keep things going, especially with two small babies underfoot and doing the best I could with what little I had to work with was just not producing the results I wanted.

My housekeeping, or lack of it, had been a point of contention between Carl and me from the beginning but now it was out of control. I would often sleep, where I could revel in my ever broadening fantasy world, until both the children were awake and many a day I wouldn't even get dressed until right before Carl was due to come home from work. The only time I cleaned house at all was when I knew that my mother or Aunt Thyra would be coming by. In the beginning Aunt Thyra would frequently drop in unannounced but soon developed the habit of either calling ahead or honking her car horn as she pulled into the driveway so I could run out to meet her. Aunt Thyra, like her mother, was also neat and most well organized and I'm sure she was more than just a little dismayed by the mess and disorganization in our house; in fact I rather think she was quite horrified by it. I'm certainly horrified as I remember it.

In my many fantasies I would be with Tom, happily married and adored or with Wesley, perhaps living in a cabin in the woods somewhere blissfully serving nature and humanity. In reality I lived just above the poverty level, had nightly arguments and experienced depression which was only marginally relieved by my fantasy retreats. When I wasn't fantasizing about being somewhere else with someone else I was crying over my shattered dream turned living nightmare. At the end of the day I was often asked what I had done all day long when the answer should have been obvious; I'd done absolutely nothing (except sleep, eat and daydream). During the first three years of my marriage to Carl we'd had two wonderful, beautiful children who deserved so much more than they got from their parents; parents who were both still such children themselves. How I managed to care for them at all over this time period I really don't know.

If things weren't bad enough our difficulties entered a new dimension when I realized how easy it was to obtain credit, and, as insane as it sounds, I rationalized my spending with the notion that if I couldn't have the *Father Knows Best* life that I wanted I could at least pretend to have it by buying things that would give the appearance of that life, even if I was the only one fooled.

The year after Jennifer was born I had finally spent so much money that we could no longer pay even a fraction of our bills and I devised yet another scheme to avoid having to face the reality I had created for myself and my family. I would pretend to have a nervous breakdown to avoid responsibility for and any repercussions from the mountain of debt. Actually I have no idea what constitutes a nervous breakdown but I had an acquaintance who spoke freely of once having been hospitalized in an upscale psychiatric ward because of her nervous breakdown and her experience sounded like fun to me. I really, really needed a break and I thought I might enjoy a month or two of stringing beads, weaving baskets and painting pictures in a solarium.

In retrospect the events that unfolded over the next few months took on a life of their own and I soon realized that I was less in control of my scheme than I thought I was. I admit to having been depressed and even occasionally very depressed and I believe that what began as pretense turned into something much more real and frightening. So much happened during this time period that I'm not sure I even have it in me to try to recall it all. The best way I know to sum up the episode is to say that after two trips to the emergency room (in as many days) and frightening the daylights out of everyone that cared about me I ended up with a referral to a psychologist and several weeks of outpatient counseling; certainly not the outcome I had aimed for.

There would be no arts and crafts or spa-like retreat nor would there be any escape from the myriad of problems. Instead I had added more trouble (and more bills) by my actions. As a result, our financial situation came more to the surface than I had bargained for when Carl had to confide in my mother and Aunt Thyra who had both been previously unaware that there were any such problems. In addition to the fact that I had now sown real seeds of mistrust into the marriage, our extended family was extremely concerned for all four of us and I was extremely angry that they had been told about our problems. I think I had wanted to punish Carl for being in my life and I guess I wanted him to bear the burden of our difficulties alone as I felt I had done for the past four years.

Things took an even more frightening twist over the next several months as I became more and more uncertain how much of what I was experiencing was pretense and how much might be the result of a real mental break. At the absolute insistence of everyone I began the prescribed outpatient counseling. Though it was a far cry from the leisurely escape I had envisioned, I did find that I was finally at least able to be honest with someone about my feelings for Carl, my relationship with my mother, the loss of my father and all the loneliness, pain and confusion I'd experienced as a child. I found all that honesty very liberating on one hand but frankly it was also a little hair-raising on the other when the counselor suggested to me that I might not be the one with the problems but that I could be acting out the problems of others in my life; like Carl and my mother.

At first I was surely puzzled by that concept but I would soon realize that the qualities that disturbed me the most in my mother; her rigidity, sullenness, anger and unpredictability were the very qualities that I absolutely hated in Carl. I was horrified to think that I might have been, even on a subconscious level, actually drawn to Carl. How could that be possible? I'd never been drawn to him at all. Could I have simply been responding to something familiar? Is that how I ended up with someone so unhealthy and so unhealthy for me because I could relate to him in a way that was at least recognizable? Why did Carl's obsession and his forcefulness prevent me from being able to say no when I wanted to so desperately? Difficult questions with even more difficult answers and of course, the counselor had to recognize my lack of self-esteem and he would end many of our sessions by telling me what a good person I was. Surely, no one had ever told me that before but instead of helping me feel better that affirmation only left me feeling more confused.

I must admit though that after a few weeks I was beginning to see myself slightly differently and when the counselor suggested that Carl and I attend counseling as a couple I was truly surprised that Carl agreed to it. I knew better than to suggest that he might have a problem but I think we both knew that we as a couple had a very big problem so we attended counseling together once a week and I continued to meet with my counselor alone on a weekly basis.

I'm not sure when I realized that the counseling we were receiving didn't necessarily have the best interest of our marriage at heart. At first I resisted the notion that we might be better off apart (though I knew it was true I just didn't have the energy at that point to even think about leaving Carl) but I was also forming a romantic attachment to my counselor and he was becoming less and less subtle as he encouraged us to divorce. One day, after about five months of counseling, while Carl was at work I packed up Andy and Jennifer and moved into the home of an older acquaintance from Oklahoma City, LeAnn who was a divorced mother with two children of her own.

Granted, my marriage to Carl was very, very unhealthy but the counsel we received was really ungodly, not Bible based, or Spirit led and LeAnn was involved in a church that bordered on being a cult. I believe it is a further indication of the Lord's enclosure that I just did not receive any of her church's ideology because she tried often to enlighten me but I had just enough of God's truth sown in me by my godly grandmother that I knew LeAnn's new age religion was farfetched. I guess that over the years I had heard just enough of the Word to recognize that some of what her church taught was a distortion and I was growing increasingly uncomfortable, not only with what I was hearing but by being in her home as well. I realize now that what LeAnn was involved in was nothing more than witchcraft; is it any wonder that I was uncomfortable in her home and with the theology she embraced? I'd say the Lord's hand was definitely upon me during my stay in that pagan environment.

Persistent as ever, Carl had called me at least once daily at LeAnn's in an effort to work things out between us. Aunt Thyra, who really seemed to like Carl, was pressuring me ever so subtly; to return home as well and finally, when

I knew the children and I had worn out our welcome at LeAnn's I agreed to return home. Carl and I reconciled, at least superficially, and even if reconciling had been the right thing to do my motives for doing so were certainly not right nor were they entirely pure or healthy. I was not anywhere near ready to attempt to provide for Andy and Jennifer financially; life would be a lot easier, at least monetarily, if Carl and I lived under the same roof again so I made what may have been the right decision for all the wrong reasons.

  I also knew I could no longer deny the fact that I would have to find some kind of a job. It had now been about six months since my 'nervous breakdown' and our finances remained precarious at best. Even thinking about the prospect of looking for a job really, really frightened me because I had never told anyone, except my counselor, about the circumstances of my marriage or about the fact that I had dropped out of high school. I surely didn't relish the thought of having to explain working at a fast food restaurant for minimum wage when I had tried to present myself as smart and together, all part of my ever increasing fantasy world. Of course, I was anything but together, I was a scared little girl with two children who desperately needed their mother yet I had nothing to give anyone, not even myself. I didn't exactly exude self confidence and I didn't know where to begin looking for a job. It wasn't just pride that was keeping me from the only jobs I felt I would be qualified for; I didn't have enough confidence to feel even capable of waiting tables! I must quickly add that I do think that self-esteem is a bit overrated in our society, preferring, instead to think in terms of Christ-esteem but in those days I possessed neither.

  When Carl and I had first moved to Tulsa I'd made friends with Carrie and Bill, a sweet couple who were just a year or two older than Carl and I and who lived in our apartment complex. I had remained friends with Carrie and

Bill after we'd moved into our house because they had a little boy the same age as Andy and the two little ones seemed to really enjoy playing together. I felt close enough to Carrie that I had confided in her about some of the problems Carl and I were having and she knew I was looking for a job. Through Bill, God miraculously provided a job for me, a real job, in an office no less, and one I could be proud to tell others about and it literally came out of the blue.

      Bill worked as a draftsman for a pipeline company and they badly needed a clerk/bookkeeper as quickly as the position could be filled due to some fast approaching deadlines. Bill literally called me one day to see if I would be interested in the job and the next day, though skeptical and full of ever present fear and self doubt, I went for my very first job interview and the day after that I reported for my first day of work. Though I had been as nervous as I could have ever been when I went to the interview I immediately liked the man I would be working for as he put me right at ease and explained that I would be taught everything I needed to know for the job.

      I know, that I know, that I know that getting that job was the first of many miracles that the Lord would perform on my behalf as part of His direct invitation to a personal encounter with Him because I'm still not sure how else I could have gotten that job. Truthfully I don't remember filling out an application but as it happened I caught on to the job very quickly and found that I actually enjoyed the work. Not only did I like the job I liked getting to know the people in the office and being treated like I might actually be capable of something worthwhile, treatment I was truly unaccustomed to and as a result I gained a sense of accomplishment that I had never experienced before. But I also received a huge wake-up call as the reality set in that even though I was now receiving my own paycheck I would not be able to support my children by myself.

Though I felt even more trapped than ever before I resigned myself to try to make the marriage work even though I really didn't want to.

Remember the question in Psalm 139: 7 "Where can I go from Your Spirit? Or where can I flee from Your presence?" I certainly was not trying to hide from God, just myself, but nevertheless that question was about to be answered for me in a profound way that I now recognize as part of God's wonderful, divine and personally tailored plan.

I spent exactly one year working for the pipeline company and during that year I shared a rather small office with one other person, Loretta. Loretta was a beautiful young lady, just a couple of years older than I, who was truly on fire for and in love with the Lord Jesus Christ! No one I had ever encountered, before Loretta, had ever asked me about my relationship with Him, or whether I even went to church and before my first week on the job was completed she had asked about both of those things. Furthermore, she seemed genuinely interested in me, my children and my problems which for the most part remained unresolved.

It's truly amazing that I was able to keep my job because I remember spending a good deal of time pouring my heart out to Loretta and being at the point of tears on numerous occasions. Loretta was a good listener and hers was the first honest to goodness godly counsel I had ever received and honestly, I wasn't quite sure how to take it. One thing was very certain to me though; Loretta was very, very genuine, she had a solid marriage, a close and loving relationship with her family, she absolutely loved her church and her relationship with the Lord was undeniably real. Loretta's life was the polar opposite of mine which was buried in debt and extremely unhappy.

I was still undergoing counseling in that very unhealthy and worldly setting and I was being encouraged to permanently leave my marriage when suddenly the counselor, with whom I had previously been a little obsessed, made a pass at me. The timing of that event was crucial because I would have welcomed that attention from this man a few months earlier but after having spent just a few short weeks with Loretta I was now bewildered and even a little angered by it. I realized that I was no longer going to benefit from the time I was spending with him and I felt an odd sense of freedom when I walked out of his office for the last time.

    Loretta invited me to attend Sunday services at her church every Friday before we left work for the weekend and I would either make up an excuse or tell her that I might show up there just to get her to back off, but months would go by before I would finally go with her. I liked to sleep late every chance I could and now that I was working I was getting up very early five days a week. Saturdays were very busy days spent shopping, cleaning and doing laundry so Sunday was MY day; my only day. I really didn't want to go to church again but I was beginning to think that Loretta did have something in her relationship with the Lord that I would probably benefit from too.

    Finally, when I was about as miserable as I could be and with my resistance at an all time low I agreed to attend a church service with Loretta. Loretta had not only talked to me about church, she had talked to me about the Lord, His love for me and my need for Him and I was becoming more and more convinced that she was right. I'd felt Him calling and drawing me almost from the very moment that she'd first begun to talk to me about Him. I knew I needed to make a big change because it was so obvious that nothing else was working for me. He saw me right where I was, knew just what I needed and I would no longer be able to attempt to flee from His presence.

Chapter 5
The Wings of the Dawn

"If I take the wings of the dawn, if I dwell in the remotest part of the sea, even there Your hand will lead me, and Your right hand will lay hold of me." (Psalm 139:9-10)

My new found church, a small congregation of about one hundred and twenty five members, was unexpected and quite different than what I had experienced in the past. I immediately found the people loving and friendly and I realized that for some reason I didn't feel quite so 'different' there. Andy and Jennifer were five and two years old by then and when I took them with me they were welcomed and loved as though they had been attending since birth. I began attending regularly and often, taking the children, most of the time, even though I was taking them alone.

One Sunday evening after church I was on my way home, alone in the car, and as I reflected on the evenings service, the fellowship, the sermon and the altar call that I had not responded to, even though I had wanted to desperately, I realized I couldn't wait any longer and I asked the Lord Jesus Christ to forgive me of my sins and I invited Him into my heart. I remember this event so vividly that I think today, more than thirty five years later, I could return to the exact spot where I was in my drive home at the moment I encountered the Lord for the very first time. I felt as though His very presence came right into the car with me. Even now remembering that moment fills me with a sense of wonder! After that amazing encounter I knew for the first time ever, that He was truly real and that He was now my Savior!

I immediately began to preach incessantly to Carl and even though I think he could see that I had made some genuine changes he wasn't ready to make those changes.

Perhaps he was waiting to see if the changes I'd made were going to be permanent before even thinking about making any such commitment himself. Carl did attend church with me occasionally, mostly if it was convenient for him or if he wanted something from me in return. For the most part though, Carl remained stiff-necked and hardhearted and our spiritual differences were now a new source of division between us.

How I wish I could say that in spite of their fathers resistance I steadfastly and joyfully continued to take our children to Sunday school and church, teaching them the fear and admonition of the Lord and helping them learn who they were in Christ but after a year or so I gave up because it just seemed too difficult a task for me to accomplish on my own. I have a very vivid memory of sitting on the floor in our living room one day with my head buried in the sofa crying out to God for a godly home and a Christ-centered marriage. I begged the Lord to help me love Carl as by now I knew a wife should love her husband. I begged for that *Father Knows Best* family that I had longed for as a child and now believed that my new found salvation should have been the key that would unlock that dream.

In my immaturity and continued selfishness my prayers for Carl during this time may have gone something like this: "Lord, save him right now, on the spot, wherever he is, whatever he is doing and change him completely so that I might find something to love in him." In other words I was demanding that God answer this prayer on my behalf so that I could have what I wanted. I was not praying for Carl's salvation because that was what was best for him. I was making it all about me and what I could gain.

Oh how I admire godly women who faithfully and single-handedly take their children to Sunday school, church and other worthwhile activities so that they will be forever grounded in the Word of God. What a tremendous example those women are setting for their husbands and children through their prayers and perseverance. I so regret not realizing the importance of that commitment because as of this writing those two children are still not entirely sure who they are in Christ. I know that God will one day gloriously reward those women who dedicate themselves to tending to the spiritual needs of their family.

    I wish I could say that after my glorious, personal encounter with the Lord I never looked back at what the world had to offer. Oh, that I might have pursued only Him after that evening in my car but I gradually abandoned my own spiritual walk and my prayers for my marriage and began a slide down a slippery slope that very nearly ended right smack dab in the very pit of hell itself! If only I had allowed Him to do a complete work in me, and there was much work to be done, but I had no idea I could give Him my every concern, fear and insecurity. I really didn't yet know to what extent He cared about the details of my life. My spirits had soared after my salvation experience but after an all too brief ascent to heaven I began a descent that would eventually take me to the very rim of Sheol.

    I believe I fell in step so easily with sin in my earlier years out of what was simply stupid, childish and just plain lost behavior; a product of the sin nature we are all born with. Yes, I knew better and was rebellious, but I was also quite naive and really couldn't comprehend the seriousness or the consequences of my actions. I didn't even really see much of my misbehavior as sin - bad behavior, maybe, but sin? No way! A lot of things looked quite different to me after my spiritual eyes were opened. Prior to the night I encountered the Lord the devil had me right where he wanted me and for twenty three years he didn't have to lift a finger to get me there. It's a place where we all are to one degree or another before we recognize our need for the Savior. Satan scarcely had to give me a second thought. Add to that the fact that I had no real expectation that I would ever be anything but a failure; an attitude the enemy of our soul absolutely revels in. No wonder he left me alone as he watched my antics with approval; I was right where he wanted me to be!

But in the spring of 1971 I'd done something the devil clearly hadn't liked and he would waste no time in plotting new and more sinister ways to destroy me. I had confessed and rejected sin, furthermore, adding insult to his injury, I had not just rejected it, I'd been cleansed of my sins and they had been forgotten. "If we confess our sins, He is faithful and righteous to forgive us our sins and to cleanse us from all unrighteousness." (1 John 1:9). Don't you know it's never a happy moment for the devil when someone who has previously so easily fallen in step with the flesh suddenly breaks out of that bondage? I'm pretty sure he didn't see that coming, not with me, anyway. He was going to fight back and for the first time he set his sights directly and squarely on devouring me. First Peter 5:8 tells Christians to "Be of sober spirit, be on the alert. Your adversary, the devil, prowls about like a roaring lion, seeking someone to devour." I just had no idea what it meant to be on the alert.

I've never liked to hear people give a lot of detail about sin when they share personal testimonies because I'm afraid that often times the devil is glorified far too much by such detail. In addition to calling attention to the devil's accomplishments (albeit limited by God Himself) there are several individuals who could be embarrassed or hurt by the recollection of some of the events that were on the horizon, including members of my own family so I'm going to limit certain details of my own testimony from this point forward. I'll just say that up until now my life had been a real Sunday school picnic by comparison!

In the beginning I had been very excited about my experience with the Lord and I was ecstatic when my entire family, including my Aunt Thyra, Uncle Joe and his wife

Kate and even my mother and mother-in-law all came to the Sunday evening service when I was baptized. I'd hoped it would be a turning point in their lives as well because only my grandmother, Uncle Joe and Kate were serving the Lord. Aunt Thyra regularly attended one of the large downtown Tulsa churches, partly for convenience but even more so because it was a social experience for her. Carl and I had attended church with Aunt Thyra on a couple of occasions after our move to Tulsa. He'd wanted no part of 'a country club' church and I hadn't really felt it suited me either. What I realize now about Aunt Thyra's church is that they just didn't seem to be producing any spiritual fruit there. I'd always felt very close to Aunt Thyra but it was really difficult for me to share the Lord with her because she was about as stiff-necked in that regard as Carl.

My mother's attitude concerning my salvation was a whole other story. Perhaps it was her memory of our shared trip to the altar several years earlier. Maybe it was the fact that she had chosen to turn her back on the Lord or just because she knew me so well, whatever her reason she was quite skeptical of my experience. In addition to being skeptical my mother's attitude regarding Christianity was "That's nice and I hope it works for you, just don't try to convert me." In fact, I seemed to encounter that attitude a lot as I tried to share my new found faith with others.

Gradually during the following year a couple of things happened that slowly started to undermine my relationship with the Lord. First, after just a few months the young pastor that had been instrumental in what little discipling I had received left the church to pastor a larger congregation in another city leaving the church without a full time pastor for several months, then, Loretta and her husband moved out of the state. I began to struggle a little because I had no mentor. Later that year my grandmother died and I was once again beginning to feel very alone and vulnerable.

But I believe that the most crucial aspect of this spiritual corrosion was the fact that after my salvation I had not received any teaching about the empowering work of the Holy Spirit, I was taught nothing about the baptism of the Holy Spirit and in fact I wasn't taught anything about the Holy Spirit whatsoever. It was as though a pair of scissors had been used to remove every reference to Him from the bible I was being taught from. In Acts 1:4-5 Jesus gives a very important word of instruction to His followers. "Gathering them together, He commanded them not to leave Jerusalem, but to wait for what the Father had promised, 'Which,' He said, 'you heard of from Me; for John baptized with water, but you will be baptized with the Holy Spirit not many days from now.'" That word of instruction, so critical for the early church was 'wait'. Even though they had no concept of the magnitude of what they would be waiting for Jesus even went on to exhort them in Acts 1:8 "but you will receive power when the Holy Spirit has come upon you; and you shall be My witnesses both in Jerusalem, and in all Judea and Samaria, and even to the remotest part of the earth."

That lack of teaching has produced for me a very personal theology regarding that word of instruction. I have come to believe that this instruction given by Jesus Himself to those first believers is just as important and applicable to all new believers as well as the entire church today. It is my firm belief that teaching about the baptism of the Holy Spirit should accompany the very earliest discipling of all new babes in Christ. I remember my own zeal and excitement as a brand new Christian and I was eager to share my personal encounter with the Lord with anyone who would listen but I lacked empowerment that I only found after I was filled with the Holy Spirit many years later.

The early Christians were instructed very specifically not to go out into the world on zeal alone; they would need something much more powerful from within; the precious Holy Spirit to strengthen, guide and direct. The power He provides not only enabled the early Christians to be Christ's witnesses to the remotest parts of the earth; He also provides power to stand against the enemy as well as much needed discernment for all they would encounter as they went out into a hostile world. That Holy Spirit power does no less for believers today, and for me, the baptism of the Holy Spirit has meant the difference between trying to do everything I know I should do under my own very limited power (and often failing miserably) and knowing that I am not alone as I stand.

It would be about ten years from the time of that first precious encounter to the time that I would be filled with the Holy Spirit and I believe that if I had been taught from the very beginning to wait for the Holy Spirit to baptize, fill and empower me that I might not have been as vulnerable as I became through the situations and circumstances that continued to plague me, as well as the new ones that were about to be thrown my way. I had entered into Christianity very enthusiastically but I had absolutely no idea what I was doing. I desperately needed power to stand against the enemy and I would need the gift of discernment even more in the days to come but the source of both would remain untapped. Even though I had been redeemed I remained a very frightened and insecure little girl and now I had a brand new enemy; I was a sitting duck just waiting to be devoured!

Recognizing what continued to be one of my greatest vulnerabilities wouldn't you know that the devil would be cunning enough to send new and even more ungodly alliances into my life? Furthermore, these new alliances would come straight out of the very church I was attending! Of course, he always knows our weaknesses very well and he'd certainly had plenty of time to observe mine. I'm sure he took detailed notes, just in case, and one of my most vulnerable areas had always been and continued to be my need for a friend and a sense of belonging. When we don't shore up our vulnerable areas through prayer the devil will invariably aim his fiery darts right at them. Perhaps Satan felt he had to be craftier now because this new onslaught didn't feel like an attack, in fact it came in the form of a brand new friendship that felt as though it was made in heaven.

I had made the mistake of not giving my deep desire for that friend I still so desperately longed for to the Lord; instead I had relied upon circumstance, as I always had, to meet the need. I may have received salvation but in this area my heart still functioned with the same level of wisdom that I might have applied in junior high. Sure enough, as circumstance would have it, I found a friend, I'll call her Cheryl, in a young woman who had been raised in my very church and who seemed as solid as a rock and I thought that I was now blessed indeed. Our friendship looked so promising, almost too good to be true; Cheryl and I were the same age, our children were the same age and our husbands shared similar interests. In the beginning I believed that Cheryl's husband, who I'll call Nick, was faithfully serving the Lord and that he would be a great friend and example for Carl. Maybe through friendship and a shared hobby, Nick would be able to lead Carl to the Lord. Surely Nick and Cheryl had been heaven sent.

I soon joined Cheryl in teaching a child's Sunday school class and Vacation Bible School. In the beginning she and Nick said and did all the right things and I gave myself to this friendship in a way I never had before. Over the next few months I was completely honest with Cheryl about myself, my past, my fears and my feelings and surprisingly she seemed to be very open with me about herself as well. I had something I'd never had before; a real live, honest to goodness best friend! If I had been better able to discern the situation I would have realized that Nick was in no way able to be a godly influence and that even though he was going through the motions of serving the Lord he was dealing with some very serious issues. For one thing, Nick had only recently returned from military service in Viet Nam and I now understand that many of his struggles originated with his experiences while there. I would soon find out that Cheryl and Nick were not who they appeared to be, in fact, their marriage was in as much trouble as Carl's and mine.

    Gradually any wholesome aspects of the friendship began to deteriorate as I spent more and more time with Cheryl. Initially Cheryl and I had really enjoyed being with each other, our children played well together and we always seemed to have a lot to talk about but we soon became bored with simple play dates, lunches and shopping trips. I soon began to lapse into some of my old habits, first, spending money I didn't have because Cheryl always seemed to have plenty of money. Then we both started drinking, first experimenting with wines at dinner and then progressing to drinking during the day. Soon we were drinking every time we were together. In the end Cheryl and I turned out to be two very miserable birds of a feather. Carl had decided after a few months that he really didn't care for Nick and Nick confided in me that he thought Carl was too possessive and completely self-absorbed, as if I didn't know that already.

    One thing led to another and soon Cheryl and I were both living truly ungodly lives. The only difference between us was that Cheryl continued to attend church, putting on a front and a different face for her family and church friends while I was too ashamed to go to church any more. Every time Cheryl and I were together we were looking for new ways to have 'fun' or add 'excitement' to our lives. We were the original 'desperate housewives' and on more than one occasion we placed our precious children in precarious situations in our pursuit of that fun or excitement. I was growing more restless and discontent in my marriage by the day and once again felt utterly trapped. I was again looking for escape from my unhappy reality, and apparently, so was Cheryl. If I learned nothing else from this relationship I did learn that true friends have each others' best interests at heart and never ask each other to do things that could be harmful, dangerous or destructive. Bad company was once again corrupting good morals. Except I'm not really sure which of us corrupted the other; I suspect that I was as bad for Cheryl as she was for me. We both were certainly deceived and I suspect that in the end she was as ashamed as I was for all our behavior.

I will draw the line at making a list of all the sinful activities that Nick, Cheryl and I ultimately involved each other in. The most horrible aspect of the whole sordid mess came to a head one evening when Carl realized the extent of our relationship after I had actually tried, without success, to drag him into the middle of a very unsavory activity. I now truly believe that on a not-so-subconscious level I had embarked on a mission to sicken Carl and drive him away. Perhaps because I had been unable to break away from him I may have thought I could so repulse him that he would be forced to leave me.

If indeed, that had been my plan it certainly worked, at least for awhile. Carl was practically in tears as he angrily threw some of his things into his car, screaming and slamming doors as he could not get out of our house fast enough. On his way out the door he said something that I have never forgotten; "and you call yourself a Christian" and that statement still haunts me today. Of course, I tried to defend myself by asking him what he could possibly know about that but make no mistake, the world knows exactly how Christians should behave and I could not have argued that there was anything even remotely Christ-like about the activities I had been engaged in for the past several months.

Within a few short weeks of that explosive exchange with Carl my friendship with Cheryl and both of our marriages were coming unraveled as the devil surely looked on with glee. Once again on the brink of divorce I had to acknowledge that most of the seven years of my marriage had been punctuated with a lot of yelling, copious tears, turmoil and mistrust. Feelings that had often been ambivalent, at best, were turning into sheer hatred, and not just on my part; I believe that Carl was beginning to hate me as well. I had not attended church in over a year and my children were not being properly nurtured or taught of the Lord. By early 1974 I was living hand to mouth with my children in the dilapidated house and incredible as it may sound, I was once again seeing the same counselor who had so misdirected me a couple of years earlier. And once again at the very top of the list of practical decisions I had to make was finding a job as soon as possible.

Through the counseling, as ungodly as it continued to be, I was at least able to take some vocational testing and was offered some advice that helped me to get a little basic direction for the future. My test scores revealed, surprisingly, that I was smarter than I thought I was; certainly smarter than I had been given credit for. I had some viable options presented to me and the vocational counselors suggested that I enroll in nursing school of all things! I had never before given any thought to becoming a nurse but it seemed like an acceptable idea. I was able to get my GED, a job as a nurse's assistant at St. John Hospital and by summer I was actually taking a couple of classes at Tulsa Junior College, now Tulsa Community College. Things seemed to be moving very fast and certainly in a direction that I'd never thought possible a year earlier. For perhaps the very first time in my entire life I thought I might actually be able to one day accomplish something worthwhile.

But, life as a single mother was very, very difficult and during this time, again for the wrong reasons, I made one last desperate attempt to repair my marriage. I had been feeling a little torn between my desire to be free from the marriage and my disdain for the stigma of divorce, but even more than that I was truly terrified of what my children and I faced financially if we remained on our own. Coming home to no gas or electricity because I hadn't been able to pay the bill was becoming a regular occurrence. Besides, my children loved their father and their lives had been turned completely upside down by the events of the last several months. I admit that I had no real intention of giving any more of myself to the marriage than I had in the past but quite frankly I needed Carl back in the house just to help make ends meet.

Carl recognized my intentions almost immediately and the arguments along with the hatred and mistrust we now had for one another reached a new level. Carl was angrier and moodier than ever before and though he had never been physically abusive I was beginning to fear that he might become so. I was on the verge of becoming physically violent myself, not that I could ever hurt Carl; he was much bigger than I was but I began provoking him just to see how far I could go before he 'lost it'. I was relating to Carl more and more like I had related to my mother as an adolescent; apparently I was still a very, very long way from growing up! I was also still secretly indulging in some of the activities that Cheryl and Nick had introduced me to and by the end of 1974 the marriage was finally and completely over.

In the end there was really only one way to summarize those nine years I spent married to Carl and that is to say that those years were a disaster waiting to happen. We had built a house upon the sand and with every storm a portion of the foundation eroded until there was nothing left. The final storm swept that pitiful little house right out to sea and not even a splinter was left standing.

    I had willingly entered into a covenant agreement without understanding just how solemn and binding the promises Carl and I had made were meant to be. A few weeks before we married I'd heard a statement; "Divorce isn't an answer, but it is a way out", and in view of our circumstances I found this statement comforting. Of course, in keeping with my *Father Knows Best* ideal for marriage I think, at least on one level, that I hadn't planned to get a divorce. I knew my family had strong feelings about divorce; even decades later Uncle Joes' divorce was rarely acknowledged but whenever it was mentioned it was always done so with connotations of disapproval. Nevertheless, I did file the statement away in my mind, just in case, because on another level I was already looking for a way out if, or more likely when, life with Carl became too unbearable.

    Carl had once again walked out of our home and this time he'd taken the initiative to end the marriage. He had enlisted an attorney, filed for divorce and then I found myself in the fight of my life because Carl had every intention of taking Andy and Jennifer from me as well. God forgive me, I truly hated this man now and there were no holds barred anymore. The divorce was nasty and the procedure drug on for nearly a year but in the end the judge, rather miraculously, ruled in my favor and I was able to retain custody of my children.

    I truly don't know how I would have reacted if the judge had actually found me to be an unfit parent. I think I might have died of humiliation had that been the outcome. For the most part though, I was quite relieved to have Carl out of the house and to have the marriage dissolved once and for all. I could breathe again without the sensation of being smothered but I also continued to be quite overwhelmed with all the responsibility that now fell squarely on my shoulders. I had long since forgotten that I had a Heavenly Father I could have run to no matter how bad life seemed. I believe if I had remembered Him my life would not have been as tormented as it had become and because I continued to forget Him things were about to get worse than I could have ever imagined even in my worst nightmares.

I began 1975 completely overwhelmed by my fulltime job at the hospital, my status as a part-time student, which I was rather enjoying, my household and mothering duties and my ever looming, ever devastating financial situation. I hadn't given much thought as to whether or not I could ever trust anyone again. I just knew I was really not all that eager to get married again. For the first time in my life I wasn't even particularly lonely; I was much too busy. I did, however, find that I was desperate for any kind of help, particularly financial help that I might be able to find. Carl only paid a minimal amount of child support. What little help he gave was never enough and I was just not able to make enough money to provide for even the most basic of needs.

In addition to being overwhelmed my emotions were right at the surface all the time and those emotions were very, very raw. I had only two or three small pictures of my father and I would stare at them and sob. I don't believe I ever missed him more or felt more cheated by his death than in those months that followed the divorce. I felt so incredibly empty. I wanted to revert back to childhood and I began sleeping with a couple of stuffed animals that I'd had since I was a baby. I was, in short, an emotional wreck and I cannot attribute anything in the natural realm to the fact that I was able to keep my sanity during that time at all; I'm sure it is only by the grace of God. I might have been lost in the remotest part of the sea but my Father knew exactly where I was as He lovingly kept His hand upon me.

Along with the financial and emotional problems I faced, ungodly alliances were coming out of the woodwork and into my life like never before. I also found, to my horror that I would say or promise just about anything to just about anyone in order to have my material needs met. I was using people right and left, and being used as well. I'm sure that everyone who knew me, even slightly could see that I put up a big (and not very convincing) front because I would frequently get very angry or just dissolve in tears with little provocation but I would pretend as much as and as long as I needed to in order to keep food on our table and the utilities turned on.

I knew several fairly well educated, professional people whose personal lives were a complete wreck and they were dragging me down with them, or was it now the other way around? Some of my new associates made Nick and Cheryl look almost like the Andersons from *Father Knows Best*. I also continued to attract some very possessive people and some of them were extremely unscrupulous as well. For example, I was awakened in the middle of the night by the estranged husband of one of my new acquaintances who, in a drunken rage had made his way to my house looking for his wife. It took several long and tense minutes to convince this man that his wife wasn't there and that I had absolutely no idea where she might be.

Another incident occurred when I went to my car one morning to find this same man sleeping it off in the back seat. I diligently kept the car doors locked after that frightening discovery and after that destructive friendship dissolved, he, at least, disappeared from my life. I didn't always know everyone who came through my house and items, usually jewelry, were stolen from me on a regular basis. One of the most ungodly relationships I had during this period nearly cost me my life when someone who was in a jealous and somewhat altered state of mind pointed a gun at me and threatened me for several terrifying minutes. That was most surely a new low and I truly now knew what it meant to scrape the bottom of the proverbial barrel.

No one will ever be able to convince me that the salvation experience I'd had a few years earlier had not been a real one. I know there is doctrine that would suggest I could not possibly have experienced true salvation and then returned to a life even more sinful than I'd left behind. I once believed that a true salvation experience would keep me secure for eternity as well. But I made a choice to walk away from the Lord when serving Him seemed too difficult. I looked back at my old life, like Lot's wife had looked back at Sodom, but the Lord refused to allow me to be destroyed by that act, even when I not only looked back, I went back to that old life of sin and despair.

When I jumped back into the fire-pit I tossed my salvation aside, I certainly didn't lose it. The prodigal son had enjoyed every privilege and luxury that his father's household had provided but he chose to walk out from under his fathers' umbrella of protection, squandered his inheritance and as a result he ended up eating from a pig sty! In the end, he also had to make the decision to return to his father's house and avail himself of his father's blessings and protection once again.

I allowed ungodly individuals into my life and home and I entered into one sinful liaison after another and now, not only was I no longer lonely, I longed to be alone. I longed for a quiet place and a quiet moment but only chaos surrounded me. Everything I did now had an ulterior motive and chaos and confusion ruled.

The shifts I had to work were not the best for my children and I tried sharing our home with another single mother and her child in hopes that we could help each other not only financially but with childcare while we worked opposite hours. The arrangement turned out to be less than desirable for oh, so many reasons. In addition to the fact our children were exposed to many things during this time that they should not have been, I also soon realized that I really didn't have enough patience to deal with other people's children. I was completely stressed, angry, bitter, hateful and just plain mean most of the time.

During the months that followed the divorce Aunt Thyra, who had been battling cancer for about a year, became seriously ill and was moved to a nursing home, where she would live out the last few months of her life. This added a new dimension of stress because she had been the only truly constant and steady person in my life. She clearly hadn't approved of the divorce but I had managed to keep her from finding out that I was living a very sinful life and she had often taken my side when my mother, ever assuming the worst in every situation, often believed things were actually worse than they really were! (When it should have been obvious that things were terrible my mother preferred to wear blinders.) Now though, Aunt Thyra, whose cancer had invaded her brain, became angry and a little mean and she wouldn't talk to me when I visited her. I finally stopped visiting when watching her deteriorate was just too difficult.

Aunt Thyra's illness also meant that my mother was coming to Tulsa much more frequently than before. I dreaded her every visit and thankfully our house was too small to accommodate her overnight so she always stayed with Uncle Joe. The stress of Aunt Thyra's illness weighed heavily on my mother who was losing her sister and only confidante. At least during this time her attention was, for once, not focused entirely on me and all I was doing wrong.

Still just having my mother in the area always made me nervous because I never knew who would show up on my doorstep when my mother happened to be there but she remained, for the most part, clueless about my lifestyle. As

I've mentioned, my mother wasn't always a good judge of character and seemed to like the 'friends' who I was forced to introduce to her. Most of the people I knew I had met at the hospital and many of them were very smart and articulate and my mother approved wholeheartedly of smart and articulate. She would not have approved of drugs and promiscuity but well-educated professionals would never involve themselves in such things, not to my mothers' way of thinking anyway.

  After Aunt Thyra's death I found myself too depressed to attend her funeral and I suspect that my mother realized that something wasn't right with me because she didn't insist that I go which was really out of character for her. Perhaps she was too ashamed to be seen with her divorced misfit of a daughter. Surprisingly though, my mother had been more supportive than I had expected when I told her, with more than just a little trepidation, that Carl and I were finally divorcing. Of course I'd blamed Carl for the collapse of the marriage and she agreed that the children and I would all be better off; she had never really liked Carl and said that she sensed the children seemed a little more relaxed since he'd moved out of the house. Actually, the children had become a little wild without Carl's iron rule and I knew they were deeply unhappy and with good reason but rather than let my mother know the truth I agreed just to keep peace. However, I once tried to talk with her about my relationship with Carl prior to our marriage and her only comment to me was that I had allowed myself to be in the wrong place at the wrong time. She believed that I got exactly what I had deserved and that would forever be the end of that discussion.

  I continue to be truly amazed that neither she nor Carl ever really knew how depraved a lifestyle I was living. I would surely have lost my children if the truth had come to the surface. My home had literally become a den of iniquity and I was eating daily from the trough just like the prodigal had done. There was a list of things that I had, over the years, stated emphatically that I would never do. I won't share the list in its entirety but the first item on that list was that I would never get pregnant before I got married. I also remember telling one of my Sunday school teachers as a young teenager that I would never drink alcohol. Of course I did both those things and then some. I had made those statements out of shear foolish arrogance. Proverbs 16:18 makes the consequences of that kind of arrogance very clear. "Pride goes before destruction, And a haughty spirit before stumbling."

Perhaps I once had made those statements thinking that I was too good for such things or maybe even that those things would never 'happen' to me. It never occurred to me to humbly commit my list of 'things I never will do' to the Lord, or to ask Him to keep me from stumbling in those things. Besides, I knew those things were wrong yet I ignored the fact that I had a responsibility to guard my own heart and mind. Feel free to use your imagination as to what other things might have been on that list; whatever you surmise may not be too far off the mark. I'd certainly broken all the commandments short of murdering someone and I had wished more than one person dead. In fact, after the divorce and during the months that followed I had a recurring dream that I had killed someone and buried the body in our basement. I would often wake from that dream wondering, at least momentarily, if in fact it might be true.

Regrettably the pride and arrogance didn't stop there as I remember one very bizarre conversation I had during this period with a coworker, about the danger of mixing Christianity with elements of her culture's false religion. What nerve I had! Here I was, my bed perched precariously at the very edge of Sheol yet ignorantly proclaiming, in so many words, that I'd been saved and it didn't matter what I was doing now. God loved me and I'd go to heaven; probably the most arrogant statement I ever made to anyone. Yet, because of a love that is quite incomprehensible my Father continued to guard me and stand by me without withdrawing His plan for my life or the work that He had prepared for me from the very foundation of the world.

In four years time I had both taken the wings of the dawn and been in the remotest part of the sea, first finding hope (and a little bit of myself) to nearly loosing it all through revisited sin and rebellion. When I gave my heart to the Lord at twenty-three that must have been His proudest moment and when I once again chose rebellion I can't imagine the grief and sorrow that He experienced. I do know that no matter where I was during these, the most painful and difficult years of my life, He was there as well. He led me without my knowing, His right hand held tightly to me no matter how I might have struggled to wriggle away.

When Satan began his assault my Father allowed him to go only so far and no further so that one day I would have a testimony. He kept me from being completely devoured by the enemy so one day I would have a ministry and so that I would be able to offer hope from His Word to others who might be in some of the same desperate situations or sin filled circumstances that I had been so wonderfully rescued from. He loved me so much that He continued to hedge me in, even when He couldn't stand what I was doing. Now, I am overjoyed by what I know about my Father's love and His presence in my life. I'm smiling because of that love even in view of the fact that I have just relived the most painful, sinful and difficult years of my life. Oh how I praise Him for His tenacity. Oh, how I praise Him!

Chapter 6
As Bright as the Day

"If I say, 'Surely the darkness will overwhelm me, and the light around me will be night,' Even the darkness is not dark to You, and the night is as bright as the day. Darkness and light are alike to You." (Psalm 139:11-12)

By the summer of 1975 my life continued to be a complete mess as darkness still threatened to overwhelm me at every turn. I was twenty-seven years old and it had been ten years since Carl and I had crafted our perverted plan. Reality was nothing like my childhood dream. Instead of the wholesome *Father Knows Best* life I had longed for I was struggling as a divorced mom; something I really don't think I ever envisioned. I was certainly not the person I had once dreamed I would become one day and life, it seemed, just kept getting more precarious every day.

Barely getting by financially had become a way of life; any relief I might have felt over the fact that I no longer had to contend with Carl on a daily basis was overshadowed by the fact that I had now become involved in what I will only describe as a truly insidious relationship.

What I got out of this relationship, besides the sensation of once again being completely smothered, was a little bit of much needed financial help but from where I stood at this point in my life the days just continued to get darker; there really was no light in sight. I'm not quite sure even now if life was more difficult or only slightly less so because I was once again settling for a relationship that wasn't right for me with someone who wasn't right for me because I remained convinced I would never have anything better. On a slightly brighter note everyone else who had been bringing ungodly influence into my life seemed to have tired of me and there was no longer the steady stream of unsavory folks flowing in and out of my home.

I had been an official college student for exactly one year. I had taken a couple of classes over the summer and was glad for the month long break before school would begin again in September. I was both excited about the fall semester and dreading it at the same time because I would begin nursing school in the fall and I fully expected that it would be quite difficult indeed and I was having doubts that nursing school was the right choice for me.

About two weeks before school would begin I awoke with a terrible toothache in a wisdom tooth that had broken through at a very awkward angle several months earlier. Now, I would no longer be able to ignore the tooth as it was producing the kind of pain that seems to make you feel like your whole body hurts; the kind of pain that prevents you from thinking of anything other than the constant throbbing.

In spite of the fact that I could have had a variety of drugs readily accessible to me I didn't keep a supply of medications on hand, having always had, for some reason, an aversion to the idea of drug use, even prescription drug use without a very good reason. That is not to say that early on I had not experimented a little with mild drug use but once I had been at a party where all kinds of drugs, in several different forms were being passed and taken rather indiscriminately. It occurred to me that most of those who were passing and taking the drugs didn't have any idea as to what they were putting into their bodies. I thank God that I had the presence of mind not to follow suit that night and that gradually after that time I became more and more disgusted by the idea. The only pain medication I had in the house was acetaminophen and I took it first thing that morning but when by nine a.m. the pain had not subsided the tiniest bit I immediately began a quest for an oral surgeon that could see me at the very earliest and thankfully, managed to get an appointment for that same afternoon. I spent the next few hours in absolute misery as

I simply waited for my appointment time to arrive. Little did I know that by the end of the day, a day that had begun so miserably, I would have a new dream for the future that would come so unexpectedly that I'm still, over thirty years later, in awe of the entire event.

When I'd made the appointment with the oral surgeon I'd been advised to have someone drive me there because I would not be able to drive myself home. So, having been driven to and from I was blissfully ensconced on the living room sofa by a little after four o'clock that afternoon. I have always had a very low tolerance for medication; anything stronger than the mildest pain pill makes me sick and it seems to take days for me to recover from anesthesia; perhaps that low tolerance explains, at least in part, why I've developed such an aversion to recreational drug use.

Never have I been happier that I took a directive to heart because truly, I could barely keep my eyes open during the trip home and once there I made it only as far as the living room sofa planning to spend at least the rest of the evening there if possible. I was quite grateful that it was Friday and Carl had taken Andy and Jennifer for the weekend; I would have the luxury of sleeping until Sunday afternoon if need be. I was still quite dopey from the anesthesia, happily pain free and relaxed as I could be on that sofa when around five-thirty there was a knock at the front door.

The sofa was directly opposite the front door so that anyone coming to the door would see the sofa, as well as anyone who happened to be lying on it. The sofa decoration on this particular afternoon was in very ragged old jeans and an even older T-shirt. The decorative accessory had 'permed' hair, making the hair even more unruly than ever (and now one side of this unruly mess was flat from the sofa while the other side stuck out at the craziest of angles). There was not a speck of makeup to be seen and in addition, there was a copious amount of drool on one side of the face, if I remember correctly. I had entered a phase over the last few months of not really caring so much about my appearance and on this day I'm afraid that I cared even less than usual. I looked simply dreadful!

My chauffeur answered the door. I had been in a sound sleep on the sofa but I forced my eyes open to see who was at the door and there stood a young man that I thought was probably the best looking fellow I had ever seen; ever. (And I still think so today.) I was quickly introduced to Rhon Ramirez, in fact our introduction had almost been an afterthought, and as quickly as he had come into my living room and my life he was gone again with the chauffeur. I remember lying back down on the sofa and thinking about him and fantasizing about him and wondering what it would take for him to notice me. Was I too far gone to even think that he would ever give me a second look? Not to mention the fact that his first impression of me may have been downright frightening. (Though he very tactfully says he doesn't remember much about it.)

I knew that the two of them would be back later that evening so going back to sleep was now out of the question; I had important things to do, like shower, put on makeup and something a little more (make that a lot more) attractive and do whatever I possibly could to my hair. I had plenty of time to be swept completely off my fcct, be married and have another child or two as I reveled in fantasy during those three or four hours while I awaited his return. When they did come back I actually got so flustered (as well as a little afraid I might make a fool of myself) that I had to leave the house and since I hadn't had anything to eat that day no one seemed to give a second thought to or even care that I was leaving. As soon as I left the house though, I realized that all I wanted to do was hurry back home so I could see him again, but sadly, he was gone when I returned home about thirty minutes later.

I should have known who Rhonnie Ramirez was; and I don't know why I'd never seen him before because we both worked the same shift at St. John, but incredibly, I had not. His parents both worked there too and I had met his sweet mother but he was a complete surprise to me that evening. I knew absolutely nothing about him and will never be able to explain the instant connection that I felt but looking back I think I was the one who was now a little obsessed. I literally thought about Mr. Ramirez every waking minute and if it is possible to do so I had fallen head over heels in love at first sight and happily we seemed to suddenly be running into each other frequently at the hospital. Though he was always polite he was obviously quite a bit less interested in me than I was in him.

A few weeks after our initial meeting I even ran into Rhonnie at Tulsa Junior College while we both were in the process of enrolling for the fall semester. Imagine my delight when a few days later, I found the love of my life and my new found soul-mate in my English class; maybe I could handle this semester after all! Of course I made a bee-line to the empty desk right beside him and claimed it (just like I'd already claimed him) as my own. I'm sure I was barely able to contain my joy over sharing this class with him; he on the other hand was merely polite and as usual, very reserved, always the gentleman. The next time the class met he had conveniently seated himself as far away from me as possible and practically broke my heart in the process. In the end I was forced to make some changes in my schedule and the English class had to be dropped.

For the next several months Rhonnie and I would continue to see each other at least once or twice a week at work and I continued to glean as much information about him as I could. Every time I saw him my heart literally skipped a beat and I would possibly have been in even hotter pursuit if I hadn't been so bogged down by the truly pitiful life I'd been leading. Not only was there still a considerable amount of despair in my personal life my worst fears concerning nursing school had been realized. It was becoming more and more obvious that I probably should have explored other options before jumping so quickly into something at someone else's suggestion.

Honestly, before my vocational counseling I had never thought, not even once, about becoming a nurse; a ballerina, yes, but never a nurse. Actually I'd always considered motherhood the highest possible calling but I'd also pondered at various times in my life that I might like to be a paleontologist (I had an amazing rock collection once upon a time), an interior decorator (whenever I visit someone's home I'm either redecorating it in my mind or gathering ideas for my own home), a forest ranger or a zoo keeper (both very serious interests for a time), but no, I'd never thought about becoming a nurse.

I do find it interesting that every time I have ever participated in any kind of test or study designed to help a person identify their motivational gift my gift has always been identified as mercy and I have no argument with that. Nurses are frequently motivated by mercy and compassion, probably the reason why my vocational testing pointed me in that direction but I should probably mention that I also have a very weak stomach and there are certain situations, situations that nurses face on a daily basis, that I simply cannot tolerate. I won't make a list of these particular situations either but let me just say that I can't eat ketchup; not because I don't like the way it tastes but because of the way it looks. Anyway, about midway through that first semester of nursing school I had an experience that I now realize was inevitable. (I was also having great difficulty keeping up with all the homework, and the math and now chemistry was way over my head.)

I wasn't getting enough sleep, I definitely wasn't spending enough time with Andy and Jennifer and I never seemed to have enough study time either. I was already seriously considering abandoning nursing altogether when one day during clinical rotation I had been helping another student dress an infected wound. As part of the process we were to pour hydrogen peroxide on the wound and when the peroxide began to bubble my partner couldn't get out of the patient's room fast enough. In fact, she didn't get out of the room fast enough and when I heard her regurgitating behind me I too started to become ill. I did, at least, make it out of the room but when our instructor caught up with us I didn't think we would hear the end of it; yes, we agreed wholeheartedly that we'd been unprofessional but unlike my partner I suspected that I would never get used to that kind of thing.

I dropped out of nursing school shortly after and have never regretted it. I felt huge relief as I made the decision to take a break from classes the next semester. There had been too many changes in my life, they'd happened all too quickly and I was glad to have a little more time with my children as well as some much needed time to breathe.

By the time 1976 began I had learned a great deal about Rhonnie and most of it should have discouraged me. For one thing, he was seven years younger than I was and since he had never been married I should have realized that my two children, one of whom was only 11 years younger than he was, might have presented more of a challenge than he might want to deal with. Yet, the fact that he had never been married was a huge point in his favor, because in comparison to everyone else I knew, Rhonnie Ramirez had very little personal baggage. No, let me rephrase that; he had no baggage to speak of at all. I shamelessly went out of my way to befriend a woman that he had been dating and from her I learned the kind of music he liked, where he lived and his birth date; all useful tidbits of information. Happily it soon came to light that this woman was not really serious about him nor was he serious about her.

Almost immediately after meeting Rhonnie I had begun to feel remorse over the way I had lived the past few years. In fact soon after our first meeting I began taking steps to end the unhealthy relationship that I was in, and this time I was completely honest about my motivation. I was not entirely sure how this would all play out but I was surprised at how little repercussion there was. I did find however that I immediately missed a small tape recorder that I had used for in-class note taking; a real annoyance but I consoled myself with the thought that it was a small price to pay for the freedom that I felt. Then, over a period of several months I would occasionally go to put on a piece of jewelry or remember a small item that I hadn't seen for a while and I realized that I been robbed once again. I was relieved to be free of this relationship because I had feared for awhile that I might be stalked, or worse, but I know that God supernaturally intervened in this situation because I can't explain its easy and almost abrupt end any other way.

However, Christmas had been very, very difficult that year, the first without Aunt Thyra and I experienced a real sense of depression over my finances and a desire just to have the holiday over with, something I had never experienced before. I looked forward to 1976, a leap year, as a wonderful opportunity to take a now or never approach to my 'relationship' with Rhonnie. Right after the first of the year I decided to have a party just so I could invite him, which turned out to be one of my lamer ideas. I made a huge effort to invite only people from the hospital that he might know but somehow a man that I didn't even know came and was much more attentive than I wanted him to be. Rhonnie apparently thought I was with this man and slipped out without anyone even noticing after about an hour. I was seriously upset by that and would have gladly asked everyone else to leave as well but my family's attempt at teaching me manners had not been a total failure.

About two weeks later I had an opportunity to go with a friend and a pilot she knew for a short flight in his small plane. I asked Rhonnie to come along but he politely declined, I went anyway and had a miserable time. By now it was February and I decided that I would make one more attempt to get this man to go out with me. The entire month of February had been unseasonably warm that year and on February 13, his birthday, I actually managed to secure a ride home from work from Rhonnie. We both worked the 3-11 shift at the hospital and because it had been such a warm and pretty day he had decided to walk to work that day. I had lent my car to someone and might truly have been marooned if he had not agreed to take me home. This required first our walking to his apartment, a mile the opposite direction, to get his car so he could then drive me home. He was apologetic but I was entirely up for the walk and that evening turned into one of the most magical I've ever experienced! Walking along Tulsa's 21st Street that night I felt more alive than I believe I ever had! By the time I arrived home we had made a date for the next day, Valentines Day! And, yes, I initiated that date too!

I had determined that I would not pursue Rhonnie indefinitely and in fact I had decided that I was only going to try to get his attention one more time. I had already been more than a little brazen and I knew there could be no doubt in his mind that I was interested in him. I was also beginning to realize that he just might not ever be interested in me. When I awoke the morning of February 14th, 1976 I was almost afraid to breathe knowing that if this date fell through there would likely not be another opportunity.

I was incredibly anxious as I waited for Rhonnie to arrive because I was very much afraid that he might not show up at all but he did and we went on our first date; a picnic. It was yet another unseasonably warm and beautiful day, probably getting well into the seventies before the day was over. I took that as a very good sign, indeed. For our picnic we journeyed to a very secluded area that only he and a few of his friends apparently knew about. Getting there was certainly tricky; we had to cross an old suspension bridge that was actually being suspended on only one side in a few places and the shallow body of water this decaying bridge crossed was several feet below. Still, every step I took getting across that old bridge was full of excitement as I literally tingled with the thrill of just being there with him.

If that weren't adventure enough when we reached our destination we decided to climb a tree that was growing at about a 45 degree angle over the shallow creek we'd just crossed. Since the tree was at an angle it was easy to climb about 7 or 8 feet up. I however, have always had a small problem climbing; actually the problem has never been so much the climb but coming back down has always made me a little unsteady. That day I came down rather quickly and suddenly by falling out of that tree about 8 feet into the creek below. (Thank God for that one or two feet of water!)

For the first second or two after the fall I was afraid to move and wondered if I could have broken my back; the breath had certainly been knocked right out of me! Then, the realization quickly flashed through my mind that we were in a very remote location. If something was broken how in the world would I be rescued; I envisioned a helicopter! My knight in shining armor of course, came immediately to the rescue and besides being completely soaked, very shaken and oh so embarrassed, I was all in one piece. I wrapped myself in the picnic blanket, we ate our lunch and then I was serenaded as the object of my affection played his violin and sang for me. No one had ever serenaded me before and I could feel myself being wrapped ever more tightly around his little finger and I loved every minute of it!

Over the next couple of weeks Rhonnie and I went on two or three dates and saw each other at the hospital almost daily. Not only had I fallen instantly in love with this man when I had met him several months earlier I was finding that the more time I spent with him the more I actually liked him and just enjoyed being with him. We laughed so freely together and he didn't even seem to be scared away by my children who were by now showing some of the classic signs of children from broken homes. They craved attention and yet were a little reserved at the same time with Rhonnie, I'm sure that they felt disloyal to Carl if they displayed any kind of affection towards him and perhaps they were even unsure as to whether or not they even wanted to have him in our lives.

Rhonnie had been the perfect gentleman and hadn't even kissed me when on February 29th I asked him to marry me, explaining that I felt more or less obligated to do so since it was Sadie Hawkins Day and all. (I absolutely love traditions and really couldn't bear the thought of breaking this one.) We both laughed but he said yes, what else was he going to say, and kissed me for the first time beneath a tree in my front yard! The world stood still in that moment and I, for one, would never be the same!

I thought that Rhonnie was perfect and I really believed that I might at least have a chance at something that I had completely missed out on until now; being in love. I really wanted to get married and though we continued to date, spending more and more time together I was sure that he considered my proposal a joke. He met my mother and she seemed to like him in her own guarded and highly opinionated way; I'm sure it helped that I had not yet told her about our age difference. I met his family and they seemed to like me, although I sensed that they were a little guarded as well, and there were lots of them, two brothers and a sister so of course, I was happy about that. All was just wonderful until Rhonnie, in fact, began in earnest to talk about marriage. I was thrilled but my mother and his family were not.

The truth of the matter is that I was downright giddy but when my mother realized how serious we were, always the realist, she immediately began to tell me every reason she could think of why our marriage would never work. I was, she explained, completely irresponsible for even considering marrying someone his age. I really did appreciate her concern for my children but from the day Carl and I had divorced her attitude had been that my life was, for all practical purposes, over. That is certainly the way she had approached her life after my father's death. In contrast, I had felt after the divorce was final that my life might one day actually begin. She grasped at all the straws she could think of; ranging from our cultural differences that existed only in her mind to the fact that since I was older it was inevitable that he would one day leave me for a younger woman. She even went so far as to tell me that if I married Rhonnie she would exclude me from her will. That led to a very angry conversation, one of many that ended by my hanging up the phone when I simply couldn't take any more.

In addition to my mother's vehement objections to our marriage Rhonnie's parents also looked upon the idea less than enthusiastically. I probably was not the girl they had envisioned for their son and one disastrous Saturday afternoon, about a month before we'd planned to marry Rhonnie and I introduced our parents to each other in a rather naïve attempt to bring everyone together and make some plans for our future but the discussion became rather heated very quickly. If memory serves me correctly my mother wasted no time in airing her objections as well as telling everyone in the room how careless, foolish and immature I was only minutes after introductions were made. The afternoon ended very, very badly. I was angry and hurt but after everyone went home Rhonnie and I had a long talk and decided to go ahead with our plans regardless of their objections.

The following week the minister we had asked to perform the ceremony, a friend from my former church, called to say that after prayerful consideration he couldn't marry us in good conscience because he just did not believe that Rhonnie loved me. He also knew that Rhonnie, though raised in a very devout Catholic family, was not even going through the motions of serving the Lord.

This man had known me right after I'd been saved and he had absolutely no idea what I'd been through the last few years but in all fairness to the situation I'm sure he discerned that I had backslidden considerably since we'd last seen each other. Of course he knew that neither one of us had sought any direction from the Lord concerning our future together. Seeking the Lord about whether or not we should get married was the furthest thing from either of our minds. Though I must admit that I did wonder myself if we were rushing into marriage a little faster than we should but I think in retrospect that I might have been afraid that if we waited Rhonnie might change his mind. I may even have backed out myself if I hadn't felt so pressured by my mother's familiar negative input. As always, my prideful attitude of wanting to show everyone that they were wrong kept me from weighing the decision I was making more carefully and today, I am so glad that things happened just the way they did.

When all was said and done Rhonnie and I were married on June 13, 1976 by a minister we literally found in the phonebook. He asked no questions and offered no counsel; Rhonnie didn't even tell his parents we were getting married. In fact, the only thing that went according to our original plans for the day was that we were able to get married at Zink Park in a truly beautiful location. The fact that hardly anyone supported our marriage was apparent when on the day of our wedding there was only my mother and one friend present. My mother, who surely would have liked to object at the appropriate time in the ceremony managed to restrain herself, at least at that particular moment. Rhonnie and I then spent our honeymoon at Tenkiller Lake camping with my children and during the course of the camping trip nearly everything we had with us was stolen! What a start we'd gotten off to.

Despite the less than ideal beginning our first month was blissful and wonderful. Rhonnie and I still seemed to enjoy each other's company, we laughed a lot and he remained, as he always has, a true gentleman, never raising his voice, getting angry or being even the slightest bit critical.

The following month my mother and Andy left for a long anticipated trip to Europe that was to be his tenth birthday gift from her. Though the tension between my mother and myself continued to mount I allowed him to go hoping that his interest in art would be stimulated and just having her out of the country for a couple of weeks would be a huge relief. The day they flew out of the Tulsa airport my mother 'accidentally' left a spiral notebook at our home containing notes she had made to herself about what to pack, things to do before leaving and several pages of a rough draft of a letter that she was writing to me outlining everything I had ever done to hurt or disappoint her. Even though Rhonnie and I were now married it was clear that she would continue to be stubbornly unsupportive. I was furious and more than just a little hurt. I thought it had all been said but apparently she was still nursing several old wounds.

My relationship with my mother was more strained than it had ever been and now another problem reared its ugly head; Carl was beginning to balk at paying child support. He'd only been regular the first few months after the divorce and his support began to dwindle considerably after Rhonnie and I started dating. Now, not only did Carl seem to be unwilling to support the children financially, my mother was adamant that she would not stand behind me if I pursued it; even Rhonnie didn't really want me to pursue the matter. I believe he felt that he would be able to take on that responsibility without any repercussions, but the truth of the matter is that we as a couple were only slightly better off financially than I had been on my own.

Our financial picture worsened when Rhonnie decided to leave his job at the hospital to pursue first one job and then another and having both plans fall apart within a matter of days. Reality was also starting to sink in concerning the children. They were wonderful children but he was not their father and they were a handful and a challenge for someone completely inexperienced in the fine art of childrearing. My new husband began to withdraw and I found myself in a very frightening position; I was head over heels in love and truly committed to our marriage but I also had two precious children and financial pressures along with the stress of adjusting to the marriage would soon create an unbearable atmosphere for us all.

Approximately three months into the marriage I made a decision that nearly broke my heart and I'm certain that this is not the decision most women in my situation would have made but truthfully I did the only thing I felt I could do under the circumstances. Especially considering that once again, I had no resources or emotional support from anyone. Once again, I was at a place in my life where I had alienated all my friends and I'd made yet another decision that caused my mother to be angry with me. In the end it seemed the only way for any of us to get any relief at all was for the children to live with their father. In desperation I allowed that very thing to happen and even though I had real misgivings I just didn't see another way. At least I knew that under Carl's roof they would be provided for materially and I didn't think they could be any worse off emotionally; our house had become something of a tomb, Rhonnie and I had stopped talking to each other and the tension had reached an all-time high.

When Andy and Jennifer moved into Carl's house the stress in our house was relieved a bit but now my mother was truly enraged and I was at such a low point myself that she and I finally had it out over the phone one day, once and for all. She reminded me she planned to exclude me from her will, threatened suicide, called me amoral and ended the conversation by telling me that my children were now in much better hands. Perhaps that statement hurt so much because I feared it might be true and for quite a few weeks after that painful discussion I dreaded answering the phone but she never called again and for the next four years we would not speak to each other at all. To add insult to injury, Carl, the person that she had grown to despise was now her greatest ally. I can't say that I blame her for reaching out to him because now that I am a grandmother I believe I might do the same in order to see my grandchildren but I don't believe I could ever do so at the expense of one of my children. (One Christmas, during those four years, I took Andy and Jennifer back to Carl's after they'd spent the night with us and my mother's car was in his driveway when we arrived.)

My first Christmas with Rhonnie was a disaster; we didn't even celebrate it and I had become so distressed and run down that I became ill and completely lost my voice for several weeks. It seemed that throughout that first year of marriage Rhonnie and I had established a very strange and uncomfortable pattern of talking to each other, as if everything was fine for one month and the next month we would not speak at all. I was even now beginning to believe that I was being punished for treating Carl, as well as a few others, so badly. I still knew so little about how God works.

In the spring of 1977 Rhonnie and I decided to sell the house that we lived in, the only thing I had gotten from my first marriage, and I felt like that could only be a positive move believing a place of our own would provide a fresh start. We listed the house with a realtor and were very pleased with the amount of equity we thought we might have but selling the house proved to be yet another disaster. First, we discovered that when Carl and I had purchased the house eight years earlier there had been a falsified termite certificate regarding the repair of some termite damage several years earlier. Next, we learned that Carl had taken a second mortgage on the house that I had never known about. In the end we got much less money than we had hoped for; we were by now just relieved to be getting out of the house with any profit at all. The darkness still seemed to be looming.

During the next two or three years, we moved twice, downsizing each time and continued the same pattern of off and on that we had established during those first critical months. The children continued to live with their father and I struggled with that as well as with the fact that I had no relationship with my mother or any extended family. I did love my husband's family though and I proceeded to pour every bit of my energy into the marriage that I so desperately wanted to succeed. The only real bright spot in my life during that time is that I at least had a job I liked and of which I could be proud. Having given up nursing school I was now pursuing a career in medical records technology and was even taking some classes again at TJC.

Strangely, even though there were so many things that seemed to be going wrong in my life at that time my self confidence did seem to be improving. I had begun volunteering as a docent at the Tulsa Zoo and I had enrolled in a zoology class taught by a woman who also taught medical students at OSU. Her class was extremely tough yet I managed to make an A and I found that my self confidence was greatly enhanced by that A. I'd also taken an algebra class, and with a little help from Rhonnie and a co-worker I made an A in that class too.

But just days before our third Christmas together Rhonnie completely blind-sided me by telling me very simply and directly that he no longer wanted to be married. This came at a time when I thought things were improving for us ever so slightly and I was not only blind-sided by his announcement I was devastated by it. I'm not even sure why I reacted the way I did because it was so out of character for me but I took the news extremely calmly. Actually I think that the instant the words were out of his mouth I just proceeded to withdraw emotionally because all I remember about the conversation is asking him if it would be possible for us to maintain the status quo at least until after the holidays.

I've never felt that the holidays were a good time to break news of that nature, I didn't want to spend Christmas alone and I was scared out of my wits about what the future might hold for me. It had never before been so clear to me that I had put all of my eggs in one basket when I had married Rhonnie. I'd walked away from any relationship I'd had with my mother, unsatisfying as it was, and had actually sent my children to live with Carl. I had always questioned that move but now at least, I would not be wondering how I would support them and myself too – I really wasn't at all sure I was going to make it.

Rhonnie agreed to wait until after Christmas was over before taking any steps to end the marriage and I determined that when the time came I wouldn't make it difficult for him. I had a good friend, Patricia, who had been a real friend and one of only two that had remained a friend during this time. Patricia had moved out of state but had recently called to tell me that she would be returning to Tulsa after the first of the year. She was single so I decided

I would contact her and talk with her about the possibility of our becoming roommates for a time.

Rhonnie and I somehow managed to get through Christmas and New Years and even though our future hadn't been discussed again I still felt that the relationship was tentative at best, and my heart and any dream I might have had for this marriage, were both truly broken. My first marriage may have been a nightmare but the pain I felt over this shattered dream was much worse than any I had every experienced or even imagined. I now had a profound realization that my egg basket was about to break scattering whatever was not already shattered. Yet it seemed that I was unable to bring myself to call Patricia because even though I had made a commitment not to make things difficult for Rhonnie I didn't want to initiate any action; that would have to be his doing. I was just numb, hurt and scared as I rang in the New Year; 1979.

St. John began the year with a campaign to improve the morale (and perhaps even the attitudes) of all of the employees. The campaign was kicked off in early January and included an employee attitude survey and a mandatory series of meetings, classes and films over a week's time. One of the films was a lecture given by a nun who had worked with alcoholics and their loved ones and I must admit that there is not a single thing that I remember about her lecture except one very important comment that she appeared to make only for my benefit. In counseling the families of alcoholics she said that it is crucial to "keep the channels of love open" while their loved one recovers.

"Keep the channels of love open." I'm not sure how many times she said that phrase or if she even said it more than once but it stuck in my mind, making a profound impression on me even as she spoke the words. "Keep the channels of love open." Would keeping a channel of love open save my marriage, I wondered? I wasn't sure how to do that but I was suddenly glad that I had not reacted to

Rhonnie's announcement about wanting to end our marriage in my usual way and I felt that I had treated him very lovingly throughout the last month but was I doing it right and was it enough? I was surely captivated by both the phrase and the concept.

It is completely clear to me that the God I had once called mine, but had then forgotten, had placed me in that auditorium on that day so I could hear those words. How awesome that He never forgets us and that He remembers our hearts deepest desires and sees us clearly even when we can't see for ourselves! Even in the darkness He sees everything that pertains to His creation. I went home that day determined to keep the channels of love open. What good would that do if my husband walked away from our marriage anyway? I wasn't sure if it would do any good at all, but I saw in that phrase a chance to do something right for a change, even if keeping the channels of love open did nothing more than allow me to get out of my marriage with some sense of dignity. That, in itself, would have been a whole new experience for me.

But for some reason I believed with all my heart that keeping the channels of love open just might save my marriage and I began to wonder if God would help me? Could I ask Him to help me? I didn't even know Him now and I had done so many unspeakable things since I had given my heart to Him. I wasn't sure He would even hear me if I asked for His help, but I did ask Him that very evening to show me those channels of love, and to teach me how to keep them open in my marriage.

It was now about the third week in January, and oddly, Rhonnie hadn't mentioned his desire or his plans to end the marriage and in fact we seemed to be getting along very well, though I feared that it was just a matter of time before the subject came up again. About a week had gone by since I had seen the film and asked God for help and I was as determined as ever to do whatever I could to keep those channels open. One weekday morning I had been at work about an hour when I was paged over the hospital intercom. I called the number only to find that I had been paged by the emergency room and that Rhonnie had been hurt at his work. I rushed to the ER to discover that he had suffered a very bad break to one of his legs, breaking not one but two bones. We barely had a chance to speak to each other before he was rushed to surgery. I didn't realize it but my prayer was about to be answered and my world was about to be forever and completely changed again.

Rhonnie spent the next week on the orthopedic floor of St. John Medical Center and I spent as much time with him as I could. It was especially nice that I was just a phone call and a few floors away since my office was on the ground floor of the same building! During this week God performed not one, but two amazing miracles for me. When I had first met Rhonnie he had been an orthopedic technician at St. John and he worked for a gentleman by the name of Pat Campbell, also someone who I considered a friend although we had never traveled in the same circles. I didn't know Pat terribly well but I had always liked his soft-spoken and unhurried manner and now he was seeing my husband at least once daily and because my father-in-law also worked at St. John I knew that Rhonnie was being very well cared for.

Pat visited Rhonnie both officially and unofficially during his hospital stay and it was during one of his unofficial visits that he brought along the lady, another hospital employee, who would become his wife in just a few months. I had seen Sandi around the hospital and had been inexplicably drawn to her but had never met her before and upon meeting her and talking with her ever so briefly I found that I instantly liked her. She is to this day one of the warmest, most genuine people I have ever met and her influence has played a big part in the fact that we are serving the Lord as Spirit-filled Christians in the wonderful church that we have attended since 1982! She would become a treasured friend indeed, but a couple of years would pass before the full impact of how the Lord would use her in my life would be realized.

In the meantime, Rhonnie was released from the hospital with a rather hefty cast, a pair of crutches and orders not to return to work for about three months. Yep, you guessed it, for the next three months I had a captive audience and a unique opportunity to keep those love channels wide open! The Lord had indeed answered the desperate prayer that I had prayed a few weeks earlier and I had one opportunity after another to keep love flowing.

The Lord was supernaturally working on Rhonnie in ways that neither of us was even remotely aware of because during that time his attitude toward me began to change noticeably. (He later told me that he thought we had turned things around before the accident, and maybe we had, but I believe this time was important for us to make that turn around complete.) I was beginning to feel close to Rhonnie again, I was beginning to trust in his love for me again, the days was looking brighter and it felt good.

You see, God wants marriages to succeed. I believe He wanted my marriage to Carl to succeed and when I refused to ask Him for help in saving it, because I didn't really want to save it, I know it broke His heart. We truly serve a God who forgives, heals and restores. Somehow the Holy Spirit used a film that was meant for another purpose entirely to get my attention and to plant an idea into my heart that would give me something to pray for in regard to a marriage that seemed doomed to fall apart.

Saving my marriage was the most important thing in the world to me on the day that I prayed that prayer but God had an even more important agenda in mind and that was saving the two people that were joined in the marriage. My Heavenly Father knew His daughter's heart even better than she did and He'd remember a little girls dream for a *Father Knows Best* family, even when I had forgotten it.

About six months after the accident Rhonnie received a financial settlement from his company and to my complete surprise he suggested that we buy a house using the settlement as a down payment. I was elated at the idea of having a house again and loved that we would have a place of our own; a place where we could start afresh. Besides, I really wanted my children back with us. There was also another even more interesting thought germinating; I wanted to have a baby very badly but I kept both thoughts to myself for awhile because I really didn't think either of those things would be possible. First, we needed to find our house and after several weeks of looking finally settled on one we liked and moved in right before Thanksgiving in1979.

We had not lived in our new home very long at all when Rhonnie suggested to me that he would like us to find a church we could attend together. That suggestion came right out of the blue and though it was completely unexpected the suggestion made me happy for reasons that I probably could never have explained at the time. Going to church as a family had once been something I'd thought I would prize and the act of attending church suggested stability and real commitment so I readily agreed.

Whenever I'd asked Rhonnie even the simplest question about his Catholic background or why Catholics did this or that he could never give me an answer. It was as though even with years of catechism none of the teaching ever took hold. My church background had been a little rigid and I had no desire to return to my former denomination so we simply took out the phonebook and picked out a church that was just a few blocks away and one that seemed to be doctrinally a very good compromise for a couple who had no idea what they believed or why they believed it.

I now see very clearly that God was doing something that neither of us would be able to comprehend for quite some time. I admit that I am not too sure I completely comprehend it yet except to say that it is so obvious that He was doing a separate yet dual purpose work in both of us. We walked one Sunday into the little church we had chosen and were immediately welcomed with open arms. We had only attended a couple of services when I suddenly found myself standing in our kitchen telling the love of my life about the night in my car when I first encountered my First Love. As I was talking to my husband something awakened inside me that I had not felt for a long time. In describing the experience to Rhonnie it seemed both a lifetime ago and as though it had just happened that afternoon. I knew in those moments that I needed God and even though I had been fully aware that He had miraculously saved our marriage a year earlier I hadn't given myself completely to Him.

Suddenly we were both so hungry for whatever God would teach us and almost immediately we were attending Sunday school and every church service, Bible study and social event we possibly could. Rhonnie gave his heart to the Lord, was baptized and before it was all said and done I ended up teaching an elementary school boys and girls Sunday school class. Rhonnie was even elected to serve on the deacon board about a year later. Yes, he was, and let me just take this opportunity to say to all the skeptics that we had known back in 1976 when we were first married that yes, in fact we are still married, blissfully and wonderfully married. (I was asked on a regular basis and by more people than I can count if I was still married to Rhonnie during those first couple of years – I don't think anyone expected our marriage to last.)

In the early spring of 1980 I finally found the right time to share with Rhonnie my desire to have a baby and for Andy and Jennifer to live with us again and he was more than receptive to both ideas. I was elated; there was just one not so slight problem. In 1974 during that very last attempt at saving my first marriage I had undergone a tubal ligation, a surgical sterilization procedure. One of the many points of contention during my marriage to Carl had been the issue of birth control.

    The father of my two older children was absolutely adamant that he didn't want any more children and though I believe with all my heart that he truly loved Andy and Jennifer I often felt that we only had them to appease me. During that last year of marriage I'd had one pregnancy scare that thankfully, turned out to be a false alarm, but in the midst of that scare Carl had made it clear that he would expect me to have an abortion if I ever got pregnant again. A year earlier I had accompanied a woman to an abortion clinic and though I wasn't terribly sure about my beliefs during that time in my life I did know this; I would never be able to have an abortion myself. I am so thankful that God's hedge of protection kept me from ever having to even consider that extreme measure because knowing that He has a unique and wonderful plan for everyone He creates I believe I would not be able to bear that kind of grief.

    Rhonnie knew that I would be unable to have children when we married and he had indicated that it didn't matter but the more we talked about the possibility of having a child together the more excited he became about that possibility. Before I ever approached the subject I had done a little research and knew that it was possible to reverse the tubal ligation and that the success rate of the reversal was increasing as techniques continued to be perfected. Now, I was faced with finding a physician who would perform the surgery and though it was still a relatively new procedure my regular doctor recommended a group of physicians that had just begun doing the surgery in

Tulsa and I was amazed at how quickly I was able to get an appointment.

After a few tests I was also amazed at how quickly the doctor scheduled the surgery. In his words, he was "cautiously optimistic"; telling me that there was possibly only a twenty percent chance that the surgery would be successful. Yet for some reason I never doubted. Oh I prayed about the situation, believe me I prayed but I had only just begun to realize what God was truly capable of. My faith journey had really only just begun yet I believed beyond what I could even begin to explain that this operation would be successful! I had even envisioned a baby in my fantasies the very first time I had met Rhonnie five years earlier.

In June, of 1980 I was wheeled into surgery for my 'reconnection'. I gave my permission to have pictures taken during the procedure because my doctors truly were the pioneers of this type of surgery in the Tulsa area. (They also happen to be some of the finest OB/GYNS on the planet!) It was all quite exciting and in late August when I went for my final post-operative checkup the doctor again reminded me not to get my hopes up restating that there was only a twenty percent chance I would become pregnant. I believe that my words to him as I walked out the door that day were "I'll see you next month".

Sure enough, by the end of September I was miraculously, wonderfully, happily pregnant and our miracle baby was scheduled to be born on May 15, 1981. Rhonnie was thrilled about the coming baby and my children were living with us again and though I had wondered how we would all adjust to so many changes I believe that things went relatively smoothly. One thing was nagging at me though and that was the fact that I missed being able to share the news of my pregnancy with my mother and even though Andy and Jennifer had been with us for a few months she continued to interact with them only through Carl.

For the first time ever I swallowed my pride and called my mother. I told her my news and made plans to visit her the following weekend. The visit was tense and true to form, she questioned me about whether or not we wanted to have a baby "What, are you crazy, do you have any idea what I went through to have this baby?" are the words that I really wanted to scream at her but I resisted and the visit ended on a fairly positive note. She visited us a few weeks later and slowly we began the work of rebuilding our relationship.

Rhonnie and I bought a big Country Squire station wagon (we called it the bowling alley) for our growing family; we even had a cat and a sheepdog! Does it get any better than that? The pregnancy though, was not without its moments. During the first trimester I experienced a bleeding episode that sent me to bed for a weekend. Then, in the fourth month I had to spend an afternoon and evening being monitored to see if I was in labor or just having Braxton-Hicks contractions. Happily the contractions turned out to be Braxton-Hicks that would plague me until the birth of the baby. I do admit that the next few months were a little stressful as we all readjusted to each other and tiring as well as I continued to work full-time but they were very, very happy months as we looked forward to the birth of our little miracle. I also very quickly grew to roughly the size of the side of an industrial sized barn!

On April 14th, one month before my due date, I was scheduled to travel to Oklahoma City with a few of my St. John coworkers. Part of my job at St. John had to do with the monitoring of the charts of Medicare patients. I would daily review the medical records of these patients to see that specific criteria were being met for their continued hospital stay and it seems that the criteria was frequently being updated. Often officials from government agencies involved with Medicare or various insurance companies would hold meetings or seminars to review these guidelines and I often attended these meetings with others from the hospital. One of the hospital administrators had offered earlier on to drive my boss and myself and another lady to Oklahoma City that morning and back that afternoon. (I was later told that when the administrator saw me he almost suggested leaving me behind – believe me, I was every bit as big as that barn and in fact, I'm still amazed that there were at least three people who saw me on a relatively regular basis who said later that they didn't even know I was pregnant.)

I remember only two things about that meeting; the lunch and the fact that I felt a little odd afterwards. I remember the lunch because it was an uncharacteristically good meal for the standard hotel meeting room luncheon - prime rib instead of the usual generic chicken dish and shortly after lunch I felt a little lightheaded and almost, but not quite, queasy. I also happened to notice that I was spotting just the tiniest little bit and oddly I wasn't terribly concerned about that but I did say a prayer that I would indeed get home without incident and the spotting stopped almost immediately.

By the time we arrived back in Tulsa I felt absolutely great. The Braxton-Hicks contractions had at times been so intense that I would have to immediately stop what I was doing and just rest until they stopped. Through the last four months the contractions had prevented me from being as active as I would have liked to have been. I was quite surprised when later that evening I felt like going to the downtown library and did a considerable amount of walking without the slightest discomfort whatsoever.

Since this was my third child I felt completely prepared for the birth and thought I knew just what to expect. I was still quite confident that the baby would not be coming for another month when I got out of bed and began to prepare for work on April 15th. Every one of my three pregnancies had been slightly different from the others in one way or another and I attributed many of the differences in this pregnancy to the fact that I was twelve years older than when I had last given birth - not exactly a spring chicken now.

Many aspects of this third pregnancy had been new to me. I'd never experienced bleeding or Braxton-Hicks contractions, nor did I remember that I'd been so exhausted in my other pregnancies and because of inactivity I gained more weight than I had with Andy and Jennifer but again, I chalked that up to the fact that I was now in my thirties. The birth of the other two babies had been very textbook and predictable; Andy after fourteen hours of labor that had been steadily progressive, but certainly not horrible, and Jennifer after approximately five hours of steadily progressive, and relatively easy, labor. In addition, Andy and Jennifer were both ten days late and both were born on a Wednesday, yes; April 15th, 1981 was also a Wednesday. Even though in my pea brain I still had a month plus an additional ten days before this baby would make an appearance, God, and the baby had a different idea and we would meet our little one face to face before the day was over.

I had a doctor's appointment that day and I was about to learn a little something. I once heard a story about a woman whose water broke in the grocery store, very conveniently in front of a display of pickles. Being a very quick thinker this woman grabbed a jar and dropped it to the floor in the exact spot where her water had broken, clever, huh? Upon hearing that story I thought that surely when one's water broke that it was similar to the breaking of a dam, need I say more? I found out around noon time that it doesn't always happen that way. Sometimes it can happen so slowly that one (OK, this one) might not realize what had happened at all.

I was sent immediately to the hospital and was told if I didn't go into labor on my own that labor would be induced before the end of the day. Rhonnie was there within the hour with all the music and games we had picked out for our labor room experience. Having Rhonnie with me was wonderful and so different from the other two deliveries. I really felt like we were a team and I knew without a doubt that my husband was every bit as excited about the birth of our baby as I was. It was pure joy! I, of course, was hooked up to all the monitors, etc. that were a part of the experience and apparently the monitors revealed that I was actually in labor but it was well after four o'clock before I felt anything even slightly different than the Braxton-Hicks contractions that had become second nature to me.

Looking back I have commented several times on the fact that if I had been at home when I first became aware that I was in labor I would probably have waited around for a bit timing contractions and since I wasn't even sure I was experiencing contractions until around five o'clock I might not have even started to the hospital until six. To make a long story short our baby, six pound, three ounce Christopher, was born at seven thirty that Wednesday evening after only about an hour and a half of anything that I would have recognized as bona fide labor!

The birth of this baby had been nothing short of one miracle after another, from his conception to God's hand of protection throughout the pregnancy and even to getting me comfortably and safely to the hospital without incident. Had the doctor's appointment not already been scheduled that day, and if my water hadn't broken that morning, I truly question whether we would ever have made it to the hospital in time. There is not a doubt in my mind that as easy as his birth was that I might have given birth in the station wagon we called the bowling alley, but again, God wanted to make sure that His hand of protection stayed in place for the entire experience because Christopher's umbilical cord was wrapped around his neck two times requiring a little extra expertise in the delivery room. Awesome, awesome, awesome! From the selection of our parents to the timing of our birth we are all so fearfully and wonderfully made!

Rhonnie was, and continues to be a wonderful, loving and attentive father (and now grandfather to four boys). His love for his child was immediately evident as he became a very 'hands on' father; changing diapers, getting up at night with the baby and always putting our needs before his own. Even my mother was impressed and though the two of them remained mostly cordial and polite to each other I could tell that her heart was softening toward my husband. We were now also very actively involved in our church where we dedicated our new baby to the Lord when he was just a few weeks old. Andy and Jennifer were both under our roof, albeit a crowded one and for a time things seemed very nearly perfect except that there were telltale signs that Andy in particular was having a little trouble adjusting to the changes taking place in his life.

At fifteen he definitely struggled with not knowing from one day to the next whether he wanted to be a child or a grownup and many times the child won over. There were behavior issues and school issues as well as the adjustment issues and they all soon became too much for all of us and he chose to return to his father's home to live and he would remain there until he finished high school. I felt that I had let him down yet at the same time I was sadly relieved. When I looked at the new baby and reflected on Andy and Jennifer's first weeks I felt so sad that they hadn't had the mother (or the father) that Christopher would have.

God had lovingly brought me out of my self imposed darkness into His marvelous light and I knew I would cling to this light with everything I had in me. There had been many times that I was surrounded by so much darkness that I couldn't see the light of day, or even a flicker of light at the end of the tunnel. In my darkest moments I thought that I would never love or be loved. I might have doomed myself to a life of loneliness and despair because I made so many mistakes and there was no way I could ever have fixed them myself and oh, how I'd wanted to.

There were times that I had allowed myself to be in unhealthy relationships, settling for so much less than what I wanted because I was in such darkness that I didn't even know there was light. Now, I realize that my entire life has been about God's desire to make me His own. I know that every situation and circumstance He allows and every godly person He has sent my way has been part of His ongoing and carefully orchestrated plan for me to know Him, to look to Him to meet my needs (and my desires) and to love Him with all my heart. And through His great love for me He would never allow darkness to overwhelm me again.

Chapter 7
Wonderful Works

"For Thou didst form my inward parts; Thou didst weave me in my mother's womb, I will give thanks to Thee, for I am fearfully and wonderfully made; wonderful are Thy works, and my soul knows it very well. My frame was not hidden from You, When I was made in secret, And skillfully wrought in the depths of the earth; Your eyes have seen my unformed substance; And in Your book were all written The days that were ordained for me, When as yet there was not one of them."
(Psalm 139:13-16)

Three years had passed since I cried out to God for help in saving my marriage and since that day He had performed many miracles in both our lives. It was just the beginning of many blessings to come when God restored our marriage, my relationship with my children and mother and most important; my faith. I would soon realize that He hadn't merely restored our marriage, He was rebuilding it, because our marriage and our walk with God was about to enter a whole new dimension. Remember, this story is really His story to write however He sees fit and He'd begun that writing when only He knew of my existence.

One of the first things I had learned to love and appreciate about Rhonnie is his gentle, unassuming nature. My husband possesses a quiet strength and after he gave his heart to the Lord those qualities of gentleness and genuine humility became even more evident. I began to realize a change in him from the very beginning of our journey together with God and I was truly in awe of what He was doing. The way Rhonnie looked at me changed and for the first time in my life I saw real love in another's eyes. He began to truly put me, our marriage and our family first and I felt that I could truly trust him the way that I had wanted so badly to trust in the beginning of our relationship. It is a miracle in itself that I had believed almost from the beginning that I could trust Rhonnie because I had stopped trusting others years before we met; probably because I had been so untrustworthy myself. Stranger still, is the fact that my trust in Rhonnie had only slightly waned when he'd announced that he wanted out of our marriage. That moment now seems as if it occurred in another lifetime, and in fact, it had, because of Gods complete and wonderful work in both our lives.

During those 'wonder' years the Lord also did something else that was not only quite amazing and unexpected but also something that would come with huge blessings even to this day. My friendship with Sandi had grown steadily from the day I had first met her years before in Rhonnie's hospital room. What I experienced with Sandi on the occasion of our first meeting was not unlike what I experienced when I met Rhonnie for the first time in that I liked Sandi immediately and felt inexplicably drawn to her as if I knew that very day that she would become a very important part of my life. I've really only had that kind of experience with very few others and every one of those people have become very, very special to me.

Sandi and Pat had married about four months after Rhonnie's accident and a short time later she had come to work in my office. I actually approached Sandi about a position that had become available and then practically insisted that my boss hire her. Our desks sat literally side by side for most of the six years we worked together and during those years we talked to each other endlessly while amazingly still managing to get our work done. I don't think either one of us could help that; the minute we saw each other in the morning words just started tumbling out and the words kept tumbling until the end of the day. Yet, we never tired of talking to one another; even after our working relationship changed when I was promoted to be her supervisor our friendship was completely unaffected.

    The better I got to know Sandi the more I liked her. For the first time in my life I had a true friend and it felt very, very good to have a friend I could confide in and with whom I could be myself. We found that we had a lot in common yet we are in some ways very different from one another but only in ways that seem to supply a sense of balance to our friendship. Our friendship is such that we can go for a very long time without interacting with one another in any way yet when we do have occasion to talk we still can't stop talking. Once we talked on the phone for three hours; this after having had no contact with each other for over a year. I guess we had a years worth of catching up to do and when we finally hung up I felt as though my left arm would be permanently bent and my left ear actually hurt.

    Initially, one of the first things Sandi and I had to talk about was where we attended church and I was a little surprised to find out that she and Pat were members of an Assembly of God church. I knew very little about the Assemblies of God but I suspected that they were Pentecostal and I was a little disappointed because my only knowledge whatsoever about the practice of speaking in tongues was that people who did it were just a little weird. (Prior to meeting Sandi all my information about speaking in tongues had come from Cheryl, need I say more?) I remember thinking to myself that Sandi seemed a bit too normal for such a thing so I decided not to hold it against her. Our friendship continued to grow and during my pregnancy we both began attending a noon Bible study at the hospital that met once a week in the office of one of the hospital administrators.

    This gentleman seemed as intrigued as I had been about Sandi's church and when he questioned her about the church and its beliefs concerning the Holy Spirit he was genuinely interested and hungry for anything and everything that God had in store for him. I, too, had been growing as a Christian and as I listened to his questions and her answers. I began to wonder if I had failed so miserably in my pursuit of godliness before because I had struggled on my own steam to do things that were impossible without the empowerment of the Holy Spirit. The church I'd grown up in and the church I'd been saved in had denied that the power of the Holy Spirit even existed and in doing so had failed their people miserably.

In my own timid way I began to seek the baptism of the Holy Spirit even though Rhonnie and I were still attending the little church in our neighborhood; another church where nothing substantial about the Holy Spirit was being taught. I soon questioned our pastor about it and his answer was that if I wanted it I could certainly ask for it but it wasn't promoted in this church because tongues were considered by some to be a little 'divisive'. About this same time I was becoming more and more aware that even though we dearly loved this sweet pastor and the people of the congregation I was finding that the teaching was not challenging us at all, Sunday school was nothing more than a coffee klatch and I was feeling a need for teaching and doctrine that was much more substantial.

The week before Christopher was born I had attended a Passover dinner with Sandi and her family at their Assembly of God church. It remains to this a day a cherished memory because up until that Saturday evening I'd had no idea that the symbolism in the Passover celebration is so deeply meaningful. I really didn't know anything about Passover except that it was Old Testament and I had no idea until that evening how relevant Passover is to the Christian church today. The young Messianic Rabbi that presided over the meal was truly anointed and I learned so much that night that I couldn't wait to share it all with Rhonnie.

I went home that evening in absolute awe of the work that had been accomplished through our Lord Jesus Christ at Calvary and how every aspect of that work had been planned for by our Lord and foretold by the Old Testament prophets. Every part of Christ's life, death and resurrection was just as God had ordained it and I was so appreciative of my new understanding of that work. After the meal Sandi showed me around the church and I remember feeling a sense of something in that place that I had never felt before. I certainly didn't observe anything weird that night and not only did the people all seem normal they were all very, very nice. That was my formal introduction to New Life Center and I left that evening being not only awed by the Passover but very impressed by the church as well.

During the year following Christopher's birth not only had Rhonnie been elected a deacon in the church we were attending, he was growing in his walk with the Lord by leaps and bounds! He was becoming as dedicated and faithful to his church as he had become to his family. I was very proud of what I was seeing in him but I was becoming more and more restless and dissatisfied with my own progress. I was still seeking the baptism of the Holy Spirit to no avail and I was hungrier than ever for deeper teaching. I was also now beginning to be disturbed by the stand that our church seemed to be taking on many social issues; particularly abortion. I soon acknowledged that I was inexplicably being pulled, not away from what had been a very loving church family but to something deeper, more meaningful and more comprehensive. I was being increasingly drawn by the Holy Spirit to Sandi's church; New Life Center Assembly of God!

I began occasionally attending Sunday evening services with Pat and Sandi in early 1982. I loved the worship and the music and Pastor Holder's teaching as I hung on every word. (After several weeks I was extremely disappointed that I had yet to even hear anyone actually speak in tongues, though.) During that summer I attended a Women's Ministries' meeting where several ladies gathered around me to pray that I be filled; still to no avail and after about thirty minutes we all gave up in exhaustion.

Soon Rhonnie began attending the Sunday night services as well. He really enjoyed New Life Center and he loved Pastor Holder immediately but he was still on the deacon board at our church and would not leave it behind easily because he was very dedicated to fulfilling that commitment. In fact, he was beginning to feel a little bit like a traitor and finally in complete desperation I tearfully told him I could do without our current church but that I didn't believe I could get along without New Life Center. He agreed (isn't God amazing?) and before the year was over we became official 'card-carrying' members of New Life Center and a new life had indeed begun for us both through that giant step of faith.

I was so incredibly hungry for everything that God had for me and I was more than just a little frustrated that I had yet to receive the baptism of the Holy Spirit. Sandi and I continued to attend the noon Bible studies and one day the gentleman who had also been seeking the Holy Spirit along with me shared a very interesting testimony. The first words out of his mouth this day was the announcement that he had indeed been filled and he was so obviously excited that even though I wanted desperately to rejoice with him I found myself jealous because I had been praying as long as he had been yet I had still not been filled. I might even have tuned him out entirely except that as he continued his proclamation I began to realize that he was describing the exact experience that I had been having for quite some time. Apparently ever so subtly the Lord had given him a syllable, just one; not even a whole word, just a syllable. He, of course had not recognized it for what it was so he tried to ignore it, thinking it was something he, himself had made up until somehow the Lord got his attention and once he spoke out the syllable the Lord added others to it and he was now, gloriously filled with the Holy Spirit.

I had been struggling with the very same situation and I was handling it the same way he had handled it, by shoving the syllable (if you could even call it that) to the back of my mind, thinking, as he had, that I'd come up with the sound on my own. The Lord had been trying to fill me with the Holy Spirit, probably from the very moment I'd first asked Him to, I just wasn't yielding to Him. When I went home that day I began to utter my syllable, the Lord added others and I too was now gloriously filled and empowered by the Holy Spirit!

I feel it bears restating that I am absolutely convinced the reason I'd failed in my Christian walk previously lies in the fact that I had not allowed the Lord to do a complete work in me by not following all the instructions laid out for me in His Word. In addition to not waiting for the empowerment of the Holy Spirit, I knew absolutely nothing about waiting upon the Lord for strength nor did I even begin to understand the concept of spiritual warfare in my earliest days as a Christian. No wonder I had been a sitting duck.

Clear instruction is given to all believers in Acts 1:4-5. "Gathering them together, He commanded them not to leave Jerusalem, but to wait for what the Father had promised, 'Which,' He said, 'you heard of from Me; for John baptized with water, but you will be baptized with the Holy Spirit not many days from now.'" I am convinced that the instruction to wait applies just as much to the new believer today as it did to those first Christians in the days prior to Pentecost. We are to wait for the infilling of the Holy Spirit because with Him comes empowerment; empowerment to witness, to walk as we should and to avoid sin. When the Holy Spirit comes we receive the power to walk away from temptation as He gently nudges us forward when needed or pulls us back in line should we start to move in a direction He isn't leading.

  I had wanted to serve the Lord so badly years earlier as a new babe in Christ, at least until things got tough, then I simply didn't know what to do when I was challenged by temptation or discouragement; it was much too easy to fall back into familiar patterns and habits of rebellion and unbelief. I would now boldly suggest to anyone who is currently in a church where there is no teaching or worse, erroneous teaching concerning the Holy Spirit to do two things: First, trust God enough to ask Him to reveal the truth to you expecting that He loves you enough to do just that. Then, see what His Word has to say about it and wait for what He has promised. "If you then, being evil, know how to give good gifts to your children, how much more will your heavenly Father give the Holy Spirit to those who ask Him?" (Luke 11:13). Our Heavenly Father wants His children to have everything available to them according to His word!

  There is everything to be gained in trusting, asking and then waiting where this important matter is concerned. I know any teaching I might have received about the Holy Spirit in the church where I'd been saved would have been very much in error. They don't believe the Holy Spirit is relevant for today yet He is as relevant today as He has been for any and every other age both before and after our generation. This issue has become a soap box of mine and now is as much a part of who I am as my fading red hair and my barely five feet, four inch stature! Besides, I don't recommend cutting those pages out of your Bible that reference the empowerment of the Holy Spirit; you just might need what is on the other side of that page one day.

  The next years continued to be filled with one change after another for our family. It is always exciting when we can see the Lord's hand at work in our lives and these were years of tremendous growth for both Rhonnie and myself. After we joined New Life Center we immediately started getting very involved. Neither of us has approached this part of our lives halfway, believing that if we were going to be members of a church we would do so wholeheartedly and we've had absolutely no regrets about that. We've been there almost every time the doors are open as we've remained involved in one area of ministry or another throughout our years there. In fact, though I'd not really thought of myself as a teacher until recently, I have to laugh when I realize that almost from the very beginning of my walk with the Lord I have been a Sunday school teacher to one age group or the other, as if I wore a badge or some other identifying label.

I began regularly attending Women's Ministries' meetings and events and in early May of 1984 I attended my first weekend retreat. One of the things that I have appreciated about New Life Center from my very first visit is the heavy presence of the Holy Spirit whenever we come together in worship, whether it's a Sunday morning service or a monthly women's meeting, and this particular event was no exception. The sweet lady that ministered at the retreat was particularly anointed and had ministered to our ladies on several previous occasions so, although she attended another church, she was practically part of our church family as well. I'd heard about the ways the Lord had used her in the past and I was quite eager to finally have the opportunity to meet her and to sit at her feet.

She was quite comfortable operating in the gifts of the Spirit and in fact as she began to speak that Friday evening she explained that even though she had known for several weeks that she would be ministering at our retreat every time she sat down to prepare the Lord had given her only one word over the weeks that she had prayed for direction and that word was 'water'. Now, I would be completely panic stricken if I were given the task of ministering to a group of ladies with only one word but she confidently and unapologetically proceeded to give us instruction as the Lord directed her.

We were to speak out as the Lord spoke to us anything He might reveal that had to do with 'water'. As Bibles were opened and concordances consulted we learned a lot about water. Water is refreshing, cleansing, thirst-quenching; an essential element in God's creation. Water can also be forceful and destructive in overabundance. Jesus, of course is the living water according to John 4:10. Our session ended with incredible praise and worship and ministry to one another.

On Saturday morning our speaker ministered again, this time with a prepared message that was equally as beneficial but the absolute highlight of the retreat happened for me during the time of body ministry that would bring our weekend to an end. New Life Center ladies really know how to minister to and pray for one another; we all know and love each other and even when someone new comes into our body they are ministered to and cared for as if they have always been a part of us. Through the years I've witnessed this over and over again and that is exactly what happened to me that Saturday morning.

After our speaker had finished her message she placed a chair in the center of the room and instructed every lady that they would at some time during the morning sit in that chair for prayer and ministry and one by one every lady did indeed sit in the chair, and at the urging of the Holy Spirit each knew when it was just her time to do so. Operation in the gifts of the Spirit was a concept that was still somewhat new and just a little intimidating to me yet when each lady was prayed for the Lord seemed to have something extremely meaningful for her.

As I waited for my own time in the chair I was beginning to get a little nervous because I had been neglecting my personal time with the Lord over the past few months. I had recently received a promotion at work which meant I was doing a lot more juggling of career and home life and I knew I was slighting the Lord. I fully expected a well deserved reprimand from my Father; instead, this is the special and highly personal word I received that morning. "I am preparing for you mothers, sisters, daughters and aunts in this body of women." I just melted into the arms of my Father because for one thing, my relationship with my mother still was not what it should have been and now I feared that my relationship with my daughter who was now a teenager might be going the same direction.

Neither of my two older children had given their hearts to the Lord and for that reason they were uncomfortable at New Life Center. In addition, even after attending New Life Center for a year and a half, I still felt a little like an outsider. This was most certainly the devil's doing, as he occasionally stirred those old feelings from childhood in hopes of keeping me somewhat isolated, because the women at New Life Center had always treated me lovingly. Since making friends had always been difficult for me I was glad that I had Sandi to cling to and she always handled my clinginess extremely well.

Instead of the expected chastisement the Lord had just reaffirmed His love for me and I went home from that retreat with a new sense of belonging and feeling very loved indeed. I continued to bask in His love but didn't think too much about the prophecy that had been given to me that day (nor the significance of the word 'water'), but I would soon do plenty of thinking about both.

On Saturday before Memorial Day in 1984 my mother had been visiting and we had gone to Philbrook Museum that day. Even though it had poured rain all day long she had decided to go home to Oklahoma City later that afternoon. That in itself was a bit unusual because my mother didn't like to drive unless conditions were absolutely pristine and though we urged her to stay overnight she'd insisted upon returning home in spite of the fact that it hadn't just rained that day, it had rained buckets and there didn't appear to be an end in sight.

Later that evening Andy and Jennifer were spending the night with their father and since it had seemingly stopped raining Rhonnie, Christopher and I decided to go to a Drillers baseball game. We had not been there very long when the rain started again and for the next thirty or forty minutes the baseball players were on and off the field for first one and then another rain delay. Finally when a torrential downpour caused the game to be called off once and for all we headed for home, completely soaked to the gills!

While my mother and I had been out in the rain that day we had made a game of counting the seconds between lightning and the subsequent clap of thunder. I believe you are supposed to multiply the number of counts by ten in order to approximate how far away in miles the lightning strike was. On our way home from the baseball game that evening Rhonnie and I continued to count the seconds between the lightning and thunder. Even as we settled into bed that night it was raining heavily and still accompanied by lots of lightning and really loud thunder; none of which seemed to be more than a mile or two away.

At two o'clock in the morning we were awakened by the storm and just minutes later there was an extremely bright flash of lightening followed instantly by an exceptionally loud clap of thunder. Still counting, I thought to myself how close that lightning must have been; close enough that our electricity had gone off. I remember thinking that I didn't want to oversleep in the morning because it was the day of New Life Center's annual Memorial Day picnic that would immediately follow the morning service. I had some last minute picnic preparations for the morning and I also needed to put laundry in the dryer so I would have something to wear to the picnic. I was now growing quite tired of rain, lightning and thunder.

I was feeling a little inconvenienced by the loss of electricity and annoyed by the loss of sleep when we heard loud and insistent knocking at our front door. I somehow knew in that moment that there would be no more sleeping for us that night. When Rhonnie opened the door I heard someone urgently shouting that our house had just been struck by lightning and our attic was already on fire. We needed to get out immediately!

Within seconds we were outside in the continuing torrential rainfall. Rhonnie had grabbed Christopher from his bed (and thankfully Christopher's security blanket that was his constant companion) and I, in a rather sheer aquamarine nightgown (at least it was one of my nicer ones) grabbed an old jacket from the closet; one that I didn't mind getting wet. I certainly didn't want to ruin one of my nicer coats. As we went out into the rain that night it suddenly became apparent that there was a raging river running about a foot deep in the street that we would have to negotiate in order to get across the street to a neighbor who had also been awakened by the storm and was beckoning us to come inside her home.

From that time forward I have believed that the gentleman that rescued us that night was an angel, along with the sweet woman who'd taken us into her home. Rhonnie said that our rescuer lived across and down the street and he had explained that he'd been up when the electricity went off so he'd stepped out to see if the whole neighborhood was in the dark. It was; and it would remain dark for several hours. I didn't know who this man was before that evening and I never saw him again but I immediately remembered the word 'water' and all it's attributes that we had studied a few weeks earlier. Not only did our rescuing angel get us out of the house safely he also literally picked me up and carried me across the street because as I stepped into the water that night the current nearly knocked me down. (In that moment keeping my nightgown where it belonged was my highest priority!)

As we entered the neighbor's house we were praying quite loudly and I've often wondered if the lady ever wondered just exactly what she had let into her house that night. As I watched our home burn from the safety of the house across the street I had one of the most incredible experiences with God that I have ever had. The fire had begun in the attic over the kitchen and the rain was coming down so hard that I wasn't initially concerned that there would be much fire damage at all. I really thought the rain would help to extinguish the fire reasoning that the roof had to already be saturated. Besides, the first things we had done when we got across the street was to call the prayer chain and then the fire department. Although, admittedly we might have placed those calls in a different order had we realized that no one else had called the fire department.

However, as we watched the fire intensify I began to realize that our house was quickly being consumed room by room and I literally began to give the contents of each room as I visualized them to the Lord. There were a few small antiques that had been my grandmother's, my mother's recital program along with several pieces of her sheet music, all the pictures and programs from my ballet recitals, several gorgeous and beautifully framed pieces of Andy's artwork, and precious pictures of the children – all items that could never be replaced.

Rhonnie and I both also began to realize that we had literally only the clothes (actually, nightclothes) on our backs and that neither of us had car keys or identification; I hadn't even had the presence of mind to grab my purse or put on my glasses. Ladies, in case of fire at least grab your purse, if at all possible, on your way out the door! As I gave the contents of our home to the Lord complete peace that really and truly does surpass all understanding came over me and I had the sensation of literally being swept up to watch the fire, not from across the street but from above as if I were watching from God's point of view. I knew in that instant that everything would be alright.

Despite the fact that we knew we'd had a large amount of rainfall that day we had not realized the severity of the storms until the firemen arrived. First, they apologized that they had taken several minutes longer to get to our fire than they would normally have taken because many of Tulsa's main thoroughfares were flooded. As the firemen worked to put out the fire Rhonnie stood on our neighbor's porch listening to their radio as reports of people trapped in cars all around the city poured in. We began to pray for the safe rescue of others instead of for ourselves. We both realized that even though our house and everything in it was going up in flames right before our eyes that all we were going to lose that night was temporal. We had walked safely out our front door and without any sense of panic whatsoever.

Watching as our house burned nearly to the ground that night I had a very personal encounter with God and I felt secure and loved as I recalled the prophecy given to me at the retreat a few weeks before. I also began to realize something that I cannot begin to explain but as I sat in that strange, dark living room; I knew that the Lord had not only prepared me a few days earlier in a very personal way for what was happening to our home, I also knew that He was going to bless us beyond measure.

For many months we had been contemplating putting our house up for sale. It was just too small for our growing family but at the time the real estate market in Tulsa was slow and interest rates had been high for quite some time. One of our neighbor's homes had been on the market for at least a year and hardly any one had even looked at it! The prospect of selling and then buying another home was not an encouraging one yet I knew also in that moment that we would be moving and I even knew where we would be moving because I had seen an area in Broken Arrow that I'd felt quite drawn to. Incredible as it sounds, in view of the relationship that I had with my mother, I'd even told Rhonnie a few months earlier that I believed that if we sold our house my mother would help us buy a new one!

The sun had barely come up that Sunday morning when Pastor Holder arrived to offer support, prayer and an immediate place to stay. Neither Rhonnie nor I had any shoes and though I had managed to borrow a shirt and pants from the woman who had opened her home to us Rhonnie was still in pajama bottoms plus an afghan that was now draped around his shoulders. We had been told to stay out of the house by the fire department until we were sure that the fire was completely extinguished and besides it was, incredibly, raining again as we left with Pastor Holder. On the way to the parsonage we learned that he had made several attempts to reach us through the night but had to turn back each time because of high water. Our Pastor is such a good shepherd and he really cares about his people so this gesture was very typical of him and it was an incredible blessing to us.

During the ride to the parsonage we also learned that our youth pastor and his family had spent several hours on top of their mobile home awaiting rescue from rising flood waters; his family included a small child and an infant. The evening had been terrifying and even tragic for so many; a few people had drowned in the floodwaters that evening and we learned that there had been at least one other house struck by lightning. And there were a large number of homes in the area that had received substantial flood damage.

As we rode the six miles to the parsonage the destruction was evident as we passed several buildings with high water marks as well as broken windows and downed tree limbs. We were so grateful that we had not experienced any terror, our rescue had been completely uneventful, and I certainly considered the loss of our house and its contents a mere inconvenience compared to what some had suffered that evening. Tulsa had experienced firsthand the terrifying, destructive and deadly attributes of water that Saturday evening. We thanked the Lord all over again for His hand of protection.

We arrived at the parsonage well before church time only to discover the church basement flooded with several inches of water. Instead of Sunday services followed by a picnic there would be a massive cleanup effort at the church. Pastor Holder was visibly shaken by all that had happened during the night as people arrived that morning, some oblivious to what all had taken place while others were already laden with donations of all kinds for those affected by the storm. One lady brought an old pair of glasses for me to use until I was able to replace my own, another even thought to bring a few essential undergarments!

My New Life Center mothers, sisters, daughters and aunts were responding to our need in such an overwhelming way that I immediately understood what God had been trying to tell me just a few weeks earlier. He loved me and would provide for me everything that I needed through these precious women. The absolute icing on the cake came when one of my dear sisters gave me this verse; "When you pass through the waters, I will be with you; And through the rivers, they will not overflow you. When you walk through the fire, you will not be scorched, nor will the flame burn you." (Isaiah 43:2).

I already knew God loved me but now I was beginning to get a glimpse of just how personal and intimate His love for me truly is. We had indeed passed through the waters without being overtaken and we had walked right out of our burning house without even smelling the smoke. I was also in absolute awe of the way the Lord had prepared the ladies of New Life Center to respond to the devastation of the storm through the word we had received corporately at our retreat. We had surely experienced another miracle!

It was Monday before we were finally able to enter what was left of our house and it seemed that despite the destruction we were, to our surprise, able to recover a few meaningful items. Christopher's bedroom had been the least damaged room in the house although everything visible was waterlogged and clearly smoke damaged to some degree. The chest of drawers in his room was intact as was his bed so I began opening the drawers to search for any salvageable clothing items; easier said than done since the water had caused the wood to swell sealing the drawers shut.

Most everything in the top two drawers were soggy and a little smoke damaged but when I opened the bottom drawer I was elated to discover that several nice studio portraits that were yet unframed and Christopher's baby books were dry and completely undamaged. Odd, because the pictures that were on the very top were in a rather thin blue paper bag now marred by a several inch long smoky mark as though flames had licked the paper yet the pictures inside didn't have a mark on them!

In our bedroom I also found my wedding ring which I had removed the night before because I occasionally experience an itchy rash caused by a reaction to soap or some other substance accumulating underneath the wide band. I also found a few other jewelry items that were important to me and in the kitchen, which was the first room to burn, as well as the most heavily damaged, I actually found the four place settings of gold flatware that Rhonnie had given me for Christmas but the most amazing and wonderful miracle of all occurred as I was searching Christopher's room for a shoe.

On Friday before the fire we'd bought a brand new pair of shoes for Christopher and on Saturday night before putting him to bed the shoes had both been placed side by side on top of his chest of drawers. One shoe remained right where it had been placed and looked good as new so I began to dig through the rubble in hopes of finding the other and hoping it too might have survived in the same good shape as its mate.

While I was looking for the shoe, which inexplicably I never did find, I heard a noise that almost sounded like a faint cough coming from under the bed. The noise startled me but I knew from the looks of the room that no human being could possibly be underneath that bed so I proceeded somewhat cautiously to take a peek. To my astonishment our beloved cat, fourteen year old Nosey had also survived both flame and waters and was now hiding under the bed. Except for being very hoarse he was none the worse for wear and we took him to Rhonnie's brother's home for safekeeping until we could reclaim him later on.

I continued to be very, very thankful for God's provision and protection during that time and because of the encounter that I had experienced with the Lord in the midst of that fire it had never even occurred to me to grieve the loss of the house. Instead, I looked forward with great expectation to our opportunity for another new beginning. The next few days were spent taking inventory of our losses, looking for a place to live and replacing essentials like glasses, driver's licenses, shoes and car keys. And yes, the house and all but a mere handful of its contents were a total loss. Miraculously neither of our cars had been in the garage that night and only one of them, the bowling alley, had a slight amount of heat damage to the front bumper.

When I returned to work a week later the ladies in my office gave me a surprise 'shower' and I went home with dishes, glassware, towels for kitchen and bath, pots and pans and even a few decorative accessories! One lady took me aside that day to tell me that I just didn't appear to be acting like a person who had just lost everything! She related to me how one of her family members had experienced substantial loss from a fire years earlier and still had not recovered from it.

I took that opportunity to tell her how graciously God had gotten us through and that without His help I most assuredly would have been in the same boat! I explained to her that there were too many ways that I could see God's hand of protection working in our lives and even though the devil meant sure destruction through that fire God caused all things to work together for good. In spite of Satan's attempts to destroy us we'd gotten out safely, our pets had gotten out safely, we had been able to salvage a few precious items and I was so very thankful that my mother had not spent the night with us that evening. She would have been panic stricken and I likely would not have had my personal encounter with God during the fire if I'd had to tend to her. I was elated to give God the praise and the glory!

Our insurance agent was very, very good to us as well and we were able to settle our claim in what seemed like a very timely manner. We had instantly made the decision not to rebuild the burned house and by now had already made a couple of trips to Broken Arrow to look around our 'new' neighborhood. When we received our insurance settlement we wasted no time in picking out a house plan that we liked and construction began by mid summer on our new home.

Now, I had always wanted two things in a house; a fireplace and I had my heart set on a two story - probably a throwback to my *Father Knows Best* dream, and the house we picked out definitely had those two things. In retrospect I do wish we'd paid a little more attention to a couple of other details; like the closets (we think they were an afterthought in the master bathroom) and the kitchen - not exactly big (in fact the fireplace may actually be bigger than the kitchen), but I loved every bit of the house when we finally moved in right after Thanksgiving in 1984.

I loved selecting the colors and the fixtures for our new home but now that we were here we realized that we had twice the house we'd had before and hardly any furniture. Almost all of our insurance money had gone into the house and the only thing substantial that we had purchased was a dining room suite. We had also purchased a bargain basement sofa and love seat that would have to do for a while but we needed beds, chairs, lamps - you name it, we needed it. For Christmas that year my mother gave us a very generous check and the memo read "For the New House" and we were told to purchase those much needed items.

My mother had even helped us with our house just as I believe the Lord had told me she would! I was thrilled with the gift and knew that the Lord had spoken to me months earlier but I was even more thrilled to realize that my mother was starting to recognize some things in Rhonnie that she admired and the gift really was symbolic of that. She would one day come to love him very, very much and even though we had taken some big steps in reconciliation we still had a long way to go in completely healing our relationship.

Rhonnie and I felt at home in our new house right away. I loved living in Broken Arrow and even the longer commutes to our jobs and our much larger mortgage didn't dampen our enthusiasm for our new home. The only drawback to those longer commutes is that I needed to get up much earlier than I had before the move; in fact I had to get up about an hour earlier. In addition to the twenty to thirty minutes needed to get from Broken Arrow to St. John Hospital, by way of the St. John Child Develop.m.ent Center, I also had to take Jennifer to Will Rogers High School in Tulsa which added an extra fifteen to twenty minutes. Provided that everyone was ready to leave on time and that timetable only truly worked if all was well on the Broken Arrow Expressway and it frequently was not.

My job was also becoming more demanding all the time and I struggled to be a good wife and mother, I'd long ago realized that I couldn't have it all but I did want to maintain some balance and morning devotion times have long been essential to me; if I focus early on the Lord I'm more likely to maintain that focus throughout the day. This attempt at staying balanced and focused led to many sleepy morning devotion times in those days. One such morning I was attempting to have what admittedly had become 'token' devotions when sure enough, I once again lost the battle to stay awake. I had gone to sleep in Rhonnie's recliner in the middle of prayer. I woke momentarily as I tried to force myself to concentrate on my prayer for the day which had at that point become simply a desperate plea to just get through the day.

As I struggled to wake up I felt, more than heard, the Lord saying to me that it was OK that I'd fallen asleep. The next thing I knew I had a very real sensation of being curled up in my Heavenly Father's arms as He lovingly cradled me, just like I had imagined many times that my own father might have done. In spite of my desire to do otherwise I realized I had held my Heavenly Father somewhat at arms length until that morning; surely because I had not known my own father and whether it had been intentional or not, I had been taught to keep my mother at arms length.

That inability to approach God as Father has been one of the biggest obstacles I've had to overcome in my Christian walk. God had been to me the awesome Creator, Sovereign and Holy and I have had absolutely no trouble at all relating to Him as all those things. I knew that He loved me, but quite honestly I found Him somewhat unapproachable as Father. I didn't know the first thing about relating to a father. The only male role model I had was Jim Anderson, my *Father Knows Best* model but if you ever watched that show, you might recall that he always wore a jacket and a tie and though always loving, his relationship with his family seemed a little formal. *Father Knows Best*, in all its unreality, had long ago represented, if only in my mind, the best a family had to offer. When I came to be a part of the family of God, I knew there was so much more. Even Jim Anderson, a model earthly father, paled in comparison to the loving Heavenly Father I grew to know more intimately that morning. On that day the Lord added a new dimension to our relationship. What a wonderful and highly personal encounter my Father provided His weary child on what would have been an otherwise routine and hectic morning!

Another time during prayer the Lord began to show me that I now had something very dear that I had prayed earnestly for years earlier and that my reality was something far better than the make believe fantasy *Father Knows Best* family I'd once dreamed of. I had a godly husband who loved me as Christ loves the church and best of all the reality of that was so much more than I had ever hoped or dreamed a marriage could be! I'd had a dream as a child but never a goal or even a plan for achieving that dream. Thank God that in the absence of my plan He had one that would give me much more than I had ever imagined. I still had a lot to learn, I still do, but He lovingly and patiently continues to teach me and I hope that as I have gotten older that He is finding me a bit more teachable. I know this, I never again want to take my Father and His amazing plan and wonderful blessings for granted nor do I ever again want to see Him as anything less that Who He is.

Since I first discovered the 139th Psalm it has been one of my favorite passages of scripture but something has always slightly bothered me about it and it is the fact that verses thirteen through sixteen always seemed like they were a little out of place! I wondered; shouldn't the psalmist have begun this chapter with these verses describing the fearful and wonderful making of a human being? He could then have progressed to his thoughts on all the things that God knew about and did for that human being.

I honestly wouldn't dare think of ever changing a word in that wonderful Psalm, just the order of the verses. But over the last year or two as I have prayed over and meditated on these verses and how I would use them in the writing of my own life story I realized something completely awesome about our Heavenly Father and I believe I know now full well why these verses are ordered as they are. It is in the very way that I have encountered Him through the years.

Certainly, one of the first things I ever learned about God was that He is all-seeing and all-knowing. If the psalmist began his writing based upon similar knowledge of God, as the all-powerful and all-knowing creator, of course he would have to begin by acknowledging that God knew everything there was to know about him. We know from the history recorded in God's word that the writer, King David, was a flawed and imperfect human being that just happened to love God with all his heart. Yes, David knew absolutely that the Lord had thoroughly searched his heart, knew his every thought, step and word. He knew and acknowledged God as his source of protection and His constant presence, even in David's darkest hour. No wonder he found all that he knew about God up to that point almost more than he could comprehend.

God has revealed so much to me about Himself and how He has fearfully and wonderfully worked in my life. The more I've sought Him and the more I've committed to do what He has called me to do the more intimate my time with Him has become. If the psalmist was having a similar experience with God I believe he became more and more aware of God's involvement in his own life as he wrote.

I'd like to imagine that the more David wrote the more personal his own encounter became as the Holy Spirit revealed more and more to him about His presence and His attention to the details of his life. There is nothing more intimate than the weaving of a child in its mother's womb, the forming of delicate inward parts and seeing in that substance the person he or she would one day become. Imagine the log He keeps of our days and how He desires to fill those days. He orchestrates the moment a child is conceived and sees that tiny frame before his existence has even been revealed to his parents. The realization of that knowledge must have flooded David's soul as he realized that same knowledge applied to him personally. How completely and how intimately God watches and pursues us; from the day we are made in secret until we draw our very last breath!

It's not just the beginning and end of our days that Our Father has ordained; it is the way we occupy our place in the world everyday in between. "For those whom He foreknew, He also predestined to become conformed to the image of His Son." (Romans 8:29). His hand has been at work in every detail from the selection of our parents, who would raise us, teach us, influence us and nurture us, as well as where and how they would do those things. He ordained who and how many brothers, sisters, aunts, uncles and cousins we would have and not only that, He paid the exact same attention to detail in their lives, right down to their very names! He's not missed a single detail!

Chapter 8
Precious Thoughts

"How precious also are Your thoughts to me, O God! How vast is the sum of them! If I should count them, they would outnumber the sand. When I awake, I am still with You." (Psalm 139:17-18)

The growing process is never a quick one and I believe that is a very good thing, for the most part, but I do wonder why it takes some people so much longer to grow up than others? Some forty year olds are selfish and childish in their thinking while there are many twenty five years olds who already seem to have lived as long as Methuselah. I only know this; the process has certainly taken a long time for me.

I'd like to think of myself as a late bloomer but that phrase tends to imply that my rate of maturity was somewhat beyond my control. The fact is I rather liked certain aspects of childhood, particularly in regard to responsibility and accountability (or should I say the lack there of). Even when I was required to behave as an adult I held on to as much childishness as I possibly could often relinquishing childish behaviors only when my fingers were pried away.

In fact, I often tell people that I grew up at New Life Center and then I quickly explain to them that no, I didn't attend church there as a child and that I've only recently grown up and the process is still very much ongoing. Thankfully, Rhonnie and I are very committed to our church and our church family and I believe that God would have to send us a certified letter before we would ever even consider leaving it for another. Among other things the teaching and the mentoring that we have received at our church has been absolutely just what has been needed to keep us going and growing in the Lord.

Pastor Holder is not one bit shy about speaking the truth in love and in addition to being such a good shepherd he is also a very good counselor.

There have also been countless opportunities for growth through service at New Life Center and we have been blessed and privileged to have been involved in so many areas of church work. Though I admit that many times I have gone into these areas of service either 'kicking and screaming' or with an attitude of pride; a very wrong attitude that has gotten me into trouble more than once. The Lord has certainly used these areas of service to teach me and even the initial attitudes that were so wrong to begin with He has used to teach me as well. That's one way I surely know that my Father is always thinking of me; He never misses an opportunity to teach me.

A few months after the fire I felt as though the Lord was preparing me to serve on the Women's Ministries board the following year. In addition to our pastors wife who has always served on the board in an advisory capacity at that time the Women's Ministries board of New Life Center consisted of a president, vice president and secretary/treasurer who were elected by the ladies in November to serve for one year beginning the following January. The fact that I felt God preparing me for this was both a baffling and exciting concept to me as I began to realize that Women's Ministries was becoming an increasingly important part of my life. My response to His still, small voice should have been to immediately begin humbling myself before Him and the ladies but instead the whole notion of actually being elected to 'serve' on the board went right straight to my head. Instead of asking the Lord for wisdom, vision, strength and help I may as well have said "Thanks, Lord, I'll take it from here."

Sure enough, just as the Lord had spoken to me I was elected president of Women's Ministries and the year proved to be challenging and even downright frightening at times. To begin with, presiding over meetings made me very, very nervous and self conscious, dealing with the ladies myriad of needs was often overwhelming and working with other personalities and temperaments was the most difficult part of all.

Add to the already weighty responsibilities of leadership things like a spring style show fundraising event - most definitely not my cup of tea, and I was almost completely done in before the year was half over. The fact that I was working full time and trying to tend to the needs of my family and home kept me fairly snowed under. It wasn't that I never asked the Lord for help I often cried out to Him, especially if I was in a jam. The problem was that I often didn't seek His help prior to stepping out on my own. Much of what I did that year was done on my own steam and I was completely burned out by year's end and ready to hand over the leadership of Women's Ministries to someone much more qualified and capable. I was more than ready to crawl back in to the woodwork for awhile.

The following year I kept a low profile, determined to keep under the radar so I wouldn't be eligible to serve on the WM board again. During that year I read a book called *The Disciplines of the Beautiful Woman* by Ann Ortlund. I don't really remember a lot about the book now - it's been over twenty years, but I do remember that it is based on the Proverbs 31 woman and reading it revived my old desire to simply be a homemaker; I was becoming increasingly unhappy and disillusioned being a working mother.

Reading the book also caused a new and surprising desire to well up inside of me as I began to dream about writing, teaching and ministering to women. I wasn't quite sure what to make of that because even though I'd just been right in the middle of a great opportunity to minister I'd felt completely unable as well as unequipped to do so. It is clear to me now that the Lord had much work to do in me before I was ready but nevertheless He was sowing seeds into my life.

Rhonnie and I had also been talking about having another baby. We had really not done anything to prevent pregnancy for at least a year or two and though nothing seemed to be happening I was confident that it would only be a matter of time before I was pregnant again and I attributed my age and stressful lifestyle to the fact that it just hadn't happened yet.

In January of 1986 I had an abnormally long and heavy period and after about ten days I made an appointment with my OB/GYN. About a week earlier the space shuttle Challenger had exploded during launch and this event had been at the forefront of the news for several days. I remember crying many a tear over that tragedy and it never occurred to me that I was more tearful than usual; after all, the entire nation was grieving. When I went to see the doctor the bleeding had begun to taper off a little but he examined me and took a blood sample, other than that, he didn't say too much except that occasionally these things happen. He certainly gave no indication that I might be experiencing anything other than a mere inconvenience. I certainly didn't think I was pregnant because my period had not been late, just long and heavy. Within another couple of days things had returned to normal and I soon forgot about the entire episode.

Rhonnie and I had reached a place financially where we felt I could leave my job at St. John and we began making preparation for that at the end of May. I was excited about the prospect of being a stay at home mom again. Christopher would be five and ready for kindergarten in the fall and Jennifer would be a senior in high school. I wanted to be there for both of them when they got home from school every day. I wanted to be a homeroom mom again. I wanted to practice being a Proverbs 31 woman, getting up early to give food to my household and sending my husband off to work with a smile on my face. I looked forward to gathering wool and flax, working with my hands in delight, girding myself with strength - you get the idea. Mostly, I was just looking forward to being free of some of the stress that had been a part of my life the last few years and bringing real balance back into my life and our home.

As April drew to a close I realized that my period was late. For some reason I was less than thrilled partly because I had more or less resigned myself to the fact that we probably wouldn't be having another child and also now a pregnancy and new baby didn't quite fit into my immediate plans. I bought a home pregnancy test but it was negative so I was somewhat relieved yet at the same time torn. I really didn't know what I wanted and my emotions seemed completely out of kilter. With emotions definitely working overtime I was edgy and tearful and after another week when my period had not come I made a doctor's appointment. On April 30th, 1986 I found out that I was indeed pregnant but, being something of an emotional wreck, I think I handled telling the news to my husband very, very badly. I don't even remember what his reaction was I just know I went to bed that evening feeling not only emotionally fragile but also with a vague feeling that something wasn't quite right.

The following day was a Friday and a work day for me and I almost had to drag myself first, out of bed, and then, to the office. As the day progressed I continued to feel both physically and emotionally unsettled and around noontime I began to bleed. I called the doctor's office and if memory serves me correctly they were not much help. I suppose they told me I could try getting off my feet for awhile but I also know there would have been nothing the doctor could have done except to just 'wait and see'. I did go home early leaving Christopher at his day care center and Jennifer at school for Rhonnie to pick up on his way home from work. I went to bed, pulled the covers over my head and cried and prayed. I had confided in Sandi before leaving work and that evening she and Pat and another couple came over to pray with us. It was a blessing and a real comfort but nevertheless the pregnancy ended in miscarriage before the day was done. It was May 1st, 1986 and the babies - I had prayed for twins, a boy and a girl to be born on my mother's December 15th birthday, were not to be.

The next week I was still bleeding heavily and when I went to see the doctor he examined me and ordered lab work just as he had done when I had experienced the bleeding episode in January. The following day I called the office as I had been instructed to let them know that I was still bleeding without any change. I returned to the office and I was absolutely devastated to learn that day that not only had I just miscarried but apparently the results of my January lab work revealed that I had been pregnant then too. In four months time I had suffered two miscarriages and I was now faced with a loss that I had never experienced before. I also now understood a level of sorrow that I had never before known. Still, I recovered fairly well. It helped that I had only a few more weeks left to work so I had something in the near future to look forward to.

The remainder of the year was really quite nice and for the most part, uneventful. I found that I truly loved being at home for my children. Many had predicted that I would become bored after having worked for so long. Some predicted that I would miss the social contact with other adults that having a job had provided but I missed neither the job, the people, the commute nor the stress. I felt quite sure I had found my niche as a homemaker and Rhonnie seemed to like having me at home, Christopher really liked it and even Jennifer seemed to enjoy having someone to come home to. Andy even moved back home for awhile and I loved having all three of my children together again under one roof.

The following year Christopher began first grade and was now in school all day and I found that I loved being a homeroom mother and getting involved in PTA; I even had time to volunteer one day a week at a crisis pregnancy center. I'd also been invited by one of my New Life Center friends to take part in a Bible study at another church that she'd been participating in throughout the past year. This opened up a whole new world and a whole new way of studying the Word for me. The Bible study was *Knowing God's Covenant* by Kay Arthur, an incredible teacher of the Word. Not only was I blessed daily by what I was learning (I discovered that I really needed a structured Bible study to keep me accountable) I was also often reminded during this time that I had a dream and a desire to write, teach and minister to women.

This would be the first of many studies by Kay Arthur, (who by now I had become quite in awe of and inspired by as well) that I would be blessed and privileged to participate in. To this day there are notations in my Bible concerning God's covenant promises made with Noah, Abraham and with His people throughout the ages, including me! This study marked the beginning of real, substantial growth in my life. I discovered that I truly love to study God's Word and that even now I am a little at loose ends during those periods from one study to the next.

By this time Sandi had also left her job at St. John to be a stay-at-home mom as well and she'd assumed the position as the leader of the ladies Bible studies at New Life Center. It was an exciting time for me because I had been asked to serve on the committee that oversaw the Bible studies and I really enjoyed being a part of, among other things, selecting the study we would do next.

I was just a little disappointed when about a year later the committee decided to do a devotional study by

Kay Arthur entitled *Lord Heal My Hurts*. Arrogantly and very erroneously, I felt that I had reached a point in my life that I no longer had any hurts, let alone any hurts that needed healing. Granted, God had done a tremendous work in me and I felt that I was being freed from hurt and sin every day so I planned to take part in the study only because it was expected of me. Dutifully, I purchased my book, gathered my highlighters and colored pencils and as I began to read I realized that there were, in fact, many hurts that needed healing. Some of those hurts were deeply buried, some superficial and then there were the most painful of all; the self inflicted wounds that I must have felt could never be healed so I had chosen to completely ignore them.

    First, I discovered that I was still deeply hurt over my father's death and the tremendous void this event had created in my life. I was forced to face all over again all the inadequacies I'd felt because of his absence; my difficult and painful childhood, my less than satisfying relationship with my mother; all circumstances that I had really had no control over but things that had been deeply hurtful to me. I also realized how deeply I still grieved over the loss of the two pregnancies. But I suffered the most grief over the consequences of my rebellious teenage years, and even more so the consequences of the many bad choices I'd made during the years after meeting Carl. High on my list of hurts was the guilt I experienced over the results of sins I committed after giving my heart to the Lord. I had many regrets and I began to realize I'd put much too much effort in wondering what might have been. How would my life have been different if I'd had a father to guide me, what if I had never gone on that first date with Carl or fallen back into sin after my first glorious encounter with the Lord?

    As the study *Lord Heal My Hurts* progressed I began to see some truly amazing and life changing truths.

The study is based on Psalm 139, a passage that has become my favorite chapter in the Bible as well as the inspiration for the telling of my own life story. It became clear almost immediately that He not only knew everything that there was to know about me He loved me in spite of everything He knew. God soon allowed me to see that not only had He hand selected my parents, He'd foreseen the untimely death of my father and the effect it would have on both my mother and myself. He knew that event, though devastating, would play a big part in the making of the woman I would become and He planned that I would one day use that event as a platform for ministry to others who'd suffered loss. I saw that event in a whole new way and realized that I had to let my Father have that hurt I'd buried through the years; only then could it truly be healed.

I learned that during my childhood and rebellious teenage years He had enclosed me with a hedge of protection that would not allow Satan to destroy me. He didn't allow me to destroy myself either! Instead I would one day realize that though I had made some very bad choices as a teenager and young adult He had forgiven me completely and that through those things I would have a platform for ministry to young women who also lacked a sense of self worth. I certainly identify with the pain of losing childhood to an untimely marriage and one that is most certainly out of God's will. I am also able to say without any reservation that there are consequences to every choice we make but He wants to use those consequences to change us, not to bring us into perpetual condemnation.

I also began to heal over the loss of the babies as I realized that God had not used the miscarriages as a means of punishment for my past sins; our Heavenly Father never treats His children that way. "He has not dealt with us according to our sins, nor has He rewarded us according to our iniquities." (Psalm 103:10). From those losses I realized that I'd acquired yet another platform for ministry. I did a lot of crying during that study but I also experienced a tremendous amount of growth as I began to realize that my life experiences had been completely overseen by the One Who created me for a purpose. He'd fearfully and wonderfully made me, He wasn't going to let me down. "Many, O Lord my God, are the wonders which Thou hast done, and Thy thoughts toward us; there is none to compare with Thee; if I would declare and speak of them, they would be too numerous to count." (Psalm 40:5).

I absolutely fell in love all over again with the Lord during this study as I began to see more clearly that there truly is none to compare with Him and none so worthy of praise and honor and glory. Allow me to say yet again that I'm in awe of Him and His wonders - the shear vastness of creation is more than I can even begin to comprehend, yet His thoughts toward me, only a small element of His creation, are too numerous to count!

If He thinks of me that often there is no doubt in my mind that He's heard every prayer and knows my hearts every desire. There is no doubt that He is continually guiding and protecting me from evil. Oh that I would think of Him half as much as He thinks of me. How I love Him and how awed I am that the Creator of the universe thinks of us more than we can count or speak of. In view of the plans that He has for His children, plans for welfare and for our future (Jeremiah 29:11) can you just imagine that He's continually thinking how to bring those plans to reality? His thoughts toward us are indeed numerous and they completely line up with His plans for us.

There remained one very large situation in my life that needed to be dealt with though. Rhonnie and I had been fairly open with each other about the lives we'd led before we met each other and he had been completely accepting of everything I had told him about myself. I'd certainly brought a large amount of baggage into our relationship and even though he'd brought comparatively little, nothing I'd told him seemed to shock or faze him. At one point we did agree that we didn't need to share every detail of our past and I was more than fine with that except for one thing.

In the very early stages of our courtship I had misrepresented a specific situation to Rhonnie. In other words, early on I'd lied to him out of fear that he would very simply be appalled if he knew the whole truth about me. I'd struggled with the fact that I had blatantly told my husband something that just was not true in order to conceal sin. I could have been the poster child for Proverbs 28:13 "He who conceals his transgressions will not prosper, but he who confesses and forsakes them will find compassion." I'd forsaken one transgression but I'd also covered it up with another.

Right around this time Pastor Holder preached a sermon series entitled "Being Set Free" that I will never forget and one sermon in particular dealt with unconfessed, hidden sin and the devastating effect that secrets of this nature can have on a person's life. It made an impact upon me because I had struggled with the secret I was keeping and it was eating slowly away at me. I knew that God had forgiven me as I had confessed the sin to Him several years before according to I John 1:9. "If we confess our sins, He is faithful and righteous to forgive us our sins, and to cleanse us from all unrighteousness." He'd even forgotten and had cast that sin as far as the East is from the West but I had not forgotten and neither had the devil.

Satan liked to remind me, not only of the sin, but that I had also deliberately misrepresented myself to a couple of people (the most important of those being my husband) through statements that I had made regarding this sin if I knew that others were involved in it. I was being blackmailed by the devil and when Pastor made the statement in the course of the sermon "confession eliminates the blackmail" I was on the edge of my seat. I felt as if he were talking directly to me yet at the same time a part of me was screaming "NO, NO, NO!!" as I reaffirmed to myself that no one would ever, ever know about this.

I felt an extra dose of condemnation because by now I knew that the Lord had placed a desire upon my heart to minister to women but I also felt a new degree of shame concerning this situation; both the sin and the fact that I was hiding something from my husband. In fact, I had already served the women of my church as their leader a year or two before this sermon was preached! I also wanted to write and teach but I didn't see how in the world I would ever be able to do this now since I really wanted to keep the secret. It really didn't seem fair that I would have to tell anyone and I especially didn't like having to remember it all over again. Even though this past sin was now completely foreign to the woman I desperately wanted to become I was afraid that my husband would be just sickened if I revealed it to him. I was surely sickened enough for the both of us and as I became more and more aware of the need to be truthful I felt so unworthy and unusable! Actually, I realize now that I must have felt like a fraud.

I left the service that Sunday in complete denial. I had dealt with the sin by almost convincing myself that it had never happened. Truth is, in addition to wishing so badly that I had never sinned in this manner I was now quite angry with Pastor Holder for calling this secret to my attention. But the absolute bottom line is that no matter how sickened I was by the sin or how far away I had gotten from it Satan knew about it and there were others who knew as well and truthfully, I was very much afraid that one day a situation might present itself and the truth would be found out. Besides I was beginning to realize that it isn't always necessary to confess absolutely everything in an open forum; at least I found a measure of relief in that.

Time went on but Pastor Holder's sermon kept ringing in my ears, I was being really convicted about keeping the secret and it was becoming more and more obvious to me that I would have to tell my husband, not only because I was being blackmailed by the enemy but now one of my children was, I feared, being lured into the same sin. I already knew that Exodus 34:6-7 says "The Lord, the Lord God, compassionate and gracious, slow to anger, and abounding in lovingkindness and truth; who keeps lovingkindness for thousands, who forgives iniquity, transgression and sin; yet He will by no means leave the guilty unpunished, visiting the iniquity of fathers on the children and on the grandchildren to the third and fourth generations." Like it or not, I knew that my only hope for complete freedom was in the confession of this secret to those who were being affected by my keeping it.

Sitting down with Rhonnie and confessing this sin and the lies I'd told to cover it up was probably one of the most difficult things I have ever done. I can't for the life of me imagine now why I expected anything less but he handled my confession so lovingly and so sweetly that I was amazed and I certainly felt freer than I had felt in a long time. I found talking with my child about my past and about what I suspected might become a problem in the next generation also relatively easy and I believe any generational strongholds were utterly destroyed that day!

Then, the Lord showed me that I needed to confess the situation to my mother, Sandi and to Pastor Holder and each time I felt a little freer and a little lighter and most of all I truly understood Romans 8:1. "There is therefore now no condemnation for those who are in Christ Jesus." I found that by being honest with my husband and others who I had deliberately deceived I could truly lay hold of the Lord's compassion, grace, lovingkindness and forgiveness.

I found so much freedom in knowing that my Heavenly Father knew me when I was at my very worst and even though His heart was breaking over my activities he continually enclosed me, hedging me in and saying "only this far and no further" to the one who was only interested in my destruction. Pastor Holder had said "confession is not a way of letting God in on a secret – He already knows our sin." Indeed, "Such knowledge is too wonderful for me; it is too high, I cannot attain to it." (Psalm 139:6). As He was hedging me in, He was not only protecting me from the hand of the destroyer, He was providing me with what would one day be yet another avenue for ministry; not just through the sin but through the circumstances surrounding it as well as the circumstances and situations that delivered me and He continues to do so today! The devil fully intended that the sin would destroy me before I was ever able to recognize God's hand at work in my life and when it did not Satan went into overdrive thinking his blackmail would surely finish me off.

Rhonnie continued to make real progress in his Christian walk and since getting past that major hurdle I hoped I was progressing as well. If nothing else I certainly felt the need to keep my progress abreast with his. Then 1988 began. Some years go by so uneventfully that I find I almost have to force myself to remember anything about them at all; I believe that experience is common to all of us. Just as some years are remembered because of outstanding or memorable events that occurred during the year; like births, weddings, special vacations or disasters. Disaster is the category heading I'll use for remembering 1988.

The year began routinely enough but somewhere along the way Rhonnie received a 'promotion' at his workplace. I placed the word promotion in quotation marks because financially we had been doing well prior to it because in addition to a regular salary Rhonnie also received a sales commission. After the promotion the commission disappeared while his work hours increased and the list of responsibilities lengthened. By the end of the year, despite the fact that I loved staying home, we both realized that I probably should find a part-time job.

At that time there was a lady attending our church who was a nurse at Saint Francis Hospital. Pat is one of the most humble and unassuming people I've ever known and I admire her greatly for oh, so many reasons. We had become very good friends because in addition to attending New Life Center, Pat also lived in our neighborhood and our little boys had played together occasionally. I had casually mentioned to Pat that I was looking for a part-time job and before that conversation was even finished she had offered me an opportunity to do what I thought would be data entry on an as needed basis. I would work two or three days a week while Christopher was in school and I could work entirely around my schedule which meant I could attend ladies Bible studies and participate in my homeroom mother and PTA activities without missing a beat. I was truly excited because that opportunity was an answer to prayer for us. Besides, it was the beginning of December and I would receive a couple of paychecks before Christmas and that would be an extra blessing.

During the first week of December I reported to work and was excited to realize that I would not be doing data entry at all but that I would be helping Pat write a text book for nurses. Pat would write several pages and I would transcribe them into a format that she had already prepared. Sometimes pages had to be rewritten several times before they were just as she wanted them but she was always so gracious and I never, ever felt pressured. I found out just how accomplished this special woman is and I also discovered an incredible strength in her as we often shared prayer needs with one another, praying for one another and bearing one another's burdens. The job was actually fun and a real blessing as well as an opportunity for me to learn some new computer skills that I would soon find valuable.

But before my first week of work was completed I reported to employee health service as every other new employee was required to do for an employee health assessment. As part of this assessment I was given a routine TB skin test. At least it was routine until three days after my initial visit when I returned to have my skin test read. Of course, before the nurse ever looked at the welt that covered most of the inside of my left arm I knew the reaction was positive. It actually wasn't the first time that had happened either; my last skin test at St. John four years earlier had showed a slight reaction but the nurse who read my test that day thought I might have had an allergic reaction to the medium used to administer the test. It had been several years since I had worked in a patient care area so she hadn't been particularly concerned about the half dollar sized red bump. Now, though there was no half dollar sized bump; the red area was more the size of five or six half dollars all laid out together. (I think it took several weeks for the welt to completely disappear too.)

As the nurse in health service looked in horror at my arm she began to question me in detail about my medical history, my family history and my work history and when I told her that I'd had a similar experience a few years earlier she began to look really concerned. She determined that the only way to be completely certain that I didn't have tuberculosis was to order a chest x-ray immediately and by now, even though I knew I couldn't possibly have TB, I was beginning to get a little concerned myself. As she was literally in the process of filling out the paper work for the chest x-ray she asked, almost as an afterthought, if there was any possibility I might be pregnant. I almost said no, but in that instant I realized that I was about three or four days late and though we had not been exactly trying any longer to have a child at that point we certainly weren't trying not to, so I told her there might be a slight possibility I could be pregnant.

Instead of the chest x-ray a blood test was ordered 'stat' and to my absolute amazement I was pregnant. Upon hearing the news I, for some unknown reason, burst into tears while the nurse looked on in bewilderment. Don't you just love what hormones can do to a woman's emotions? I'm not sure why her next move surprised me but it not only surprised me, it upset me even further. She ordered me to report to an on-site counselor for what I can only surmise was a mental health evaluation!

In one day's time I had learned I might have TB, learned I was pregnant and had a mini-emotional breakdown complete with brief visit to counselor (who I later decided may have been the only rational one of the three of us because he completely understood my outburst in view of the other miscarriages combined with the scare of the positive TB test). I honestly can't remember how the rest of the day went but I do remember that it was December 13, 1988 and when I returned to my little corner of someone else's office I couldn't help notice the slogan on the coffee mug on the desk. It read "I'd Rather be Forty Than Pregnant". I was forty and pregnant, quite exhausted and by now completely in awe of the circumstances that had brought this fact to my attention and the God that had orchestrated them and I suspect I must have gone home and crawled directly into bed.

I wasted no time in calling our family physician and within just a couple of days I had an appointment with a highly recommended high-risk pregnancy specialist who I felt quite sure was also God ordained in my life at this special time. Because of my history and my age I was given an injection to be repeated in ten days, that the doctor hoped would sustain the pregnancy after lab work determined that my hormone levels were a little lower than they should have been. He seemed cautiously optimistic about the pregnancy and I was optimistic too except for the fact that my optimism was a little guarded because of the past miscarriages. I knew one thing that I would do immediately; I would have as many people pray over me and the baby as possible!

I believe that my visit to the doctor was around the eighteenth of December and I went home from that visit feeling very encouraged. I felt that because of the unusual circumstances surrounding the early discovery of the pregnancy that God had His hand on the baby. I truly wanted to believe that the pregnancy would be successful and in my mind I had calculated an August due date. Thinking 'pink', we'd already picked out a girl's name, Emily Catherine, when we were expecting Christopher and we both still loved the name. I actually felt quite good; I'd never experienced morning sickness with any of my pregnancies and was only just slightly more fatigued than usual. I was looking forward to Christmas and the next visit to the doctor in another ten days.

I only worked two or three short days the week before Christmas but on December 23rd I began to experience a familiar and unwelcome slight discharge. My mother arrived later that day to spend the holiday and seemed quite a bit less than excited when I shared our news, news that I would not have shared with her at all quite yet except that I was trying to stay off my feet as much as possible; I was also trying desperately to think positively in regard to the outcome of the pregnancy. I took her reaction in stride and though I spent most of the day in the recliner the remainder of it was for the most part uneventful.

On Christmas Eve morning I got out of bed and almost immediately I began to bleed heavily. My specialist, who had been very supportive and understanding had instructed me to call him immediately if I were to have any signs that I might miscarry so I took him at his word and called his answering service. Of course, there was no one in the office on Christmas Eve and about an hour later one of his associates, a young woman, returned my call and seemed almost annoyed that I'd called when there was absolutely nothing that could be done. I believe her exact words were "obviously this is not a good pregnancy". I was angry at her lack of concern and devastated as the bleeding continued to increase with every hour. I knew I was miscarrying and along with the heavy bleeding I was experiencing no small amount of pain.

Of course, my mother had been there the entire time and she had already expressed her feelings which mirrored the young woman doctor's. She actually asked me later that evening if I'd been crying because of the physical pain or from the disappointment. I really wanted to scream at her for being so insensitive but I had accepted her way of thinking long before that day. The truth is, I could no more have explained to her that day that both the physical and emotional pain I was experiencing were almost unbearable.

Because of the history we shared I'd learned to keep a stiff upper lip with my mother years earlier and for the remainder of her visit I was about as stoic as I have ever been grieving privately in one corner while Rhonnie grieved privately in another. Both my mother's presence and the depth of our disappointment kept us from grieving together and I felt completely alone that Christmas Day even surrounded by my family. This was the miscarriage that occurred right before *The Land Before Time* incident; honestly, sitting in that movie theatre about a week later was the first time I'd felt the freedom to cry as I had wanted to from Christmas Eve forward.

I approached the new year with a commitment that I would not be undone by our latest loss but that I would forge ahead and do whatever needed to be done to have a normal pregnancy and a healthy baby. Two and a half years earlier, after the second miscarriage, I had received a verse from a woman at our church, 1 Samuel 2:3; "There is no one holy like the Lord, indeed, there is no one besides Thee, nor is there any rock like our God." In view of the context of 1 Samuel 2, I determined that this verse served as nothing short of a promise from God that we would, indeed be blessed with another child one day. I'd believed for some time that Christopher was our Samuel but I reasoned that because Hannah had other children after her miracle baby that I would certainly have another child too. Why else would I have been given this verse? I felt encouraged as I made an appointment with my OB/GYN to see what could be done to prevent another miscarriage when, not if, I became pregnant again.

The doctor performed a number of tests in hopes of identifying my problem and suggested that there were a number of possibilities ranging from minor to major but indicated that most could be dealt with. I believed with all my heart that once we knew the problem it would be easily fixed. I was baffled by the fact that prior to the first miscarriage I had gotten pregnant easily and except for minor problems when I carried Christopher my pregnancies, for the most part, had been relatively uneventful. I reasoned though, that perhaps part of my problem was due to the fact that I was by now forty years old; that would at least explain why getting pregnant was not as easy as it once had been. That didn't explain why suddenly I couldn't carry a baby more than a couple of weeks. My enthusiasm for finding a solution to the problem waned as each test that had been performed indicated no abnormalities and no problems. This went on for several months while one by one, the doctor ruled out every problem he had suspected.

Finally, in April when I had my last appointment with the doctor he suggested something that I was truly unprepared to hear. He'd found nothing either in my lab work or other tests that indicated any kind of abnormality. He could not explain why I was unable to sustain a healthy pregnancy and he had done everything he knew to do. It was at that point that he suggested that Rhonnie and I were most likely genetically incompatible. That would explain why I was able to become pregnant but not able to sustain the pregnancy to term. There was really only one way to determine for certain if, indeed, this was the case and that would require extensive, and expensive genetic profiling; tests that were not covered by our health insurance. My head was spinning when I left that appointment. Rhonnie and I had, after all, had a very healthy and completely normal child. After prayerful consideration we decided not to have the testing and to simply trust God to do whatever He sovereignly determined would be for our best and His ultimate glory and I still believed with all my heart that we would have another child.

  Christopher was by now eight years old and an active second grader so we were very busy with his activities as well as our own. Rhonnie and I remained very active at our church and I continued to work part-time and serve on the PTA board at Christopher's school. I remember those days fondly and realize in the recalling of them that they passed far too quickly. I also now realize that I probably was not as much fun to live with as I would have liked to have been. For one thing I was still learning the principles of spiritual warfare and the disappointments of the failed pregnancies were weighing far too heavily upon me. I tried very hard not to dwell on those pregnancies, preferring instead the notion of thinking positively about the future, but I failed to recognize the work of the enemy and how he used such things as disappointment and past failures to defeat me and to keep me from living victoriously every day before the Lord and others.

In fact, one of the words in the English language that I began to hate with a passion is the word 'endure'. Yes, I know endurance has its place; we are to "run with endurance (patience) the race that is set before us", (Hebrews 12:1). Mark 13:13 tells us that "the one who endures (perseveres) to the end, he shall be saved". But truly I prefer both the words patience and perseverance to simply enduring which suggested to me at the time that life is simply to be endured until something better comes along. I wanted to be patient and I definitely wanted to persevere but where living is concerned I prefer to live victoriously, overcoming the enemy's every assault! Of course I now fully understand that sometimes enduring is the only way to overcome and achieve victory.

On April 30th of 1991 I took a pregnancy test that would be my last positive one. On the following day, May 1st and exactly five years to the date from my first known miscarriage, I miscarried again. Over the years I had begun to feel as though I were in an episode of the old TV series *The Twilight Zone* in which a poor sailor was doomed to be in one shipwreck after another. He would be rescued every time but every ship that rescued him would ultimately be wrecked sending him back into the sea to await rescue by yet another doomed ship. Oddly, this last miscarriage produced a healing of sorts by causing me to realize that having another child was probably not God's plan for me and at the same time I would also come to realize that even though I would not ever see or hold those four (or five?) children on this earth that He still had a sovereign plan for them as He does for each and every one He creates. Once again, I grieved considerably but for the first time I felt a sense of closure and healing after the tears were shed.

The year before the last miscarriage, when Christopher was nine years old an opportunity presented itself that my husband seemed to eagerly embrace. The couple who had faithfully taught New Life Center's children's church had decided to take a much needed and well deserved break and Rhonnie informed me that we would be taking over the children's church ministry for a time. This is definitely one of those times I went kicking and screaming into ministry. I really did not want to teach children's church. I had become so busy working (again, though still only part-time) and taking care of my family that my dreams for writing, teaching and ministering to women had been placed so far back in my mind that I hardly even thought of them.

My Heavenly Father continued to teach and nurture this daughter in the way that only He could do. He had taken over where my grandmother had left off years earlier to "Train up a child in the way he should go, even when he is old he will not depart from it." (Proverbs 22:6). I had served as the Vice President of Women's Ministries recently but I wasn't exactly doing anything ministry oriented at the moment. I hadn't been able to talk Rhonnie out of children's church and finally resigned myself to the fact that I would be a warm body there, maybe I'd do crowd control if necessary, while he did the teaching; after all, he was the one who got us into this.

Almost immediately, very likely the first Sunday we were actually in children's church, God's Gang is what it was named in those days, the Lord began to speak to me about giving my all to the ministry that I was called to at the moment. I've found through the years that even when the Lord has called us to something in the future that many times we are just as called to situations we might find ourselves in during the present. Besides, there was still much work to be done in me as well. I felt as though I had matured a lot in my walk with the Lord and I certainly had come a long way but I still had a very long way to go (and I dare say I'm not there yet). Yes, children's church was just the place that this child needed to be.

I think I learned more about applying God's word to my life during those days than I had ever learned before. I've really never been one to do things halfway and soon after we had taken over God's Gang it was enrollment time for summer Kids Kamp at Turner Falls and I knew right away that I would be going to camp with our children. I felt very strongly that as their minister, camp counselor should also be part of my role, and even though I dreaded it I began immediately prayerfully preparing myself for the inevitability of it. One thing I did look forward to was the fact that at nine years of age Christopher would be able to attend Kids Kamp and I looked forward to being part of his first church camp experience. Besides, I had now grown to love the kids in God's Gang very much.

That summer about thirteen children from New Life Center went to camp with Stan, our sweet, young youth pastor and myself as the counselors. Christopher seemed excited about going to camp and though eight had been the official age to begin attending camp we'd purposely not sent him the year before feeling that he might still be a little young for four nights and five days away from home. Rhonnie and I now were both confident that Christopher could go to camp, especially since I would be accompanying him. I looked forward to observing him interact with the other campers and he had given his heart to the Lord when he was six years old so I was also excited about the experiences he would have with the Lord and other young believers. I would be constantly on the lookout for him, observing, without being observed, whenever possible.

We arrived at Turner Falls around 1:00 p.m., the official arrival time for all campers. After checking in, settling into dormitories and a short orientation our session of camp was officially underway. Of course, the first thing I did after settling my girls was to find Christopher and meet his counselor. I wanted to know who would be ministering to my son during this special week. I can't remember why our youth pastor was not the counselor for the boys from our church but he was not and instead of the gentle and easygoing Stan that Christopher had come to know quite well, a very regimented, almost military man would be my son's counselor and I instantly had a feeling this would never work. I'm sure this man was very loving and a very good counselor but I could tell from the moment that I observed him with Christopher that they would clash, and clash they did. By supper time I found myself on the lookout for my son with every step I took; not so I could interact with or observe him but so I could quickly make sure he didn't see me because I'd already seen him enough to know he was miserable and I knew he wouldn't miss an opportunity to let me know it.

About 6:30 the next morning I happened to observe my little son in a line of other young boys following their counselor single file, all with bibles in hand on the way to somewhere for morning devotions and I cringed because they were the only ones out at that hour and I believe they were actually marching. By breakfast it was all over for Christopher Ramirez, he desperately wanted to go home and by lunchtime I was becoming equally as desperate to have him go, yet all the while explaining to him there was no way for him to leave and that no, neither his father nor one of his grandmothers would be coming to get him. I prayed for strength and endurance like never before. About an hour after breakfast I was approached by the camp director because two of the children from our church had had a family emergency and their parents would be coming to get them that afternoon. I was to make sure that the children were all packed up and ready to go. The family lived across the street from us and I immediately began the process of making arrangements for Christopher to return home with them.

The parents arrived just before dinner time and they graciously agreed to take Christopher and Rhonnie would take him to Sandi's for the remainder of the week because he had to be at work very early every morning. I was just about to breathe a sigh of relief when as Christopher was in the process of getting into the car one of the kids closed the car door on my son's hand! At that point I was more than ready to just get in the car and head home with them. I was worn out from lack of sleep; arrival day activities had kept us up very late the night before. I was slightly irritated at both the counselor that had spoiled Christopher's first camp experience and by the fact that our son would miss out on the rest of the week. And now I had to send him home hurt and upset. He was crying and so was I, and by now I truly wondered what I was doing there, but I didn't have time to wonder long because by the time they drove away it was dinner time and then there would be just enough time to shower, make sure the girls were cleaned up and all of us dressed for the evening service.

I had enjoyed the service the night before very much, despite the obvious distraction, the evangelist was a skilled and talented ventriloquist who shared an anointed message geared for kids but also thought provoking for adults. God's Word tends to be that way as it contains something for everyone, no matter what their level of spiritual maturity. Though still tired and a little distracted I was a lot more relaxed when I arrived at the second evening's service and found myself much more readily entering in to first the fun part of the service as we all got our 'wiggles' out and then the praise and worship. I once again enjoyed the evangelist's ministry and many of the children responded to the altar call.

I suddenly realized that I was really enjoying the camp experience without having to worry about my son and I also began to realize that this camp experience was for me and me alone; Christopher's camp experience would have to wait another year. This week was an opportunity for me to redeem an experience I'd had as a young teenager when I'd gone to church camp and had wasted the entire week chasing a boy that didn't even know I was alive. As usual, I'd managed to alienate anyone that had tried to befriend me and I'd gone home feeling miserable and sorry for myself. This time I would go home exhausted, yes, but bubbling over with the joy of the Lord and with new commitment to the ministry I was presently involved in.

Rhonnie's job with a once very successful company was becoming less and less lucrative with every paycheck and I was finding that I needed to work more but Pat's book was nearly finished and she didn't need me as often as she had needed me initially. During this time our finances were repeatedly stretched and strained and yet the Lord always provided wonderfully. Our finances never seemed to quite work out on paper yet our needs were always miraculously met. Pat had arranged for me to work part time doing data entry for another department in the hospital and my time was spent between the textbook and the accounting department. This was a huge blessing because as my job with Pat came to an end work in the accounting department increased and soon I was working as many hours a week as I wanted. I was still able to be home when Christopher got home from school and I was still also able to schedule my work days around PTA and ladies Bible study and the extra money helped us through some very rough spots.

Finally Rhonnie realized that his job situation would not improve and in addition to the fact that the money had dwindled over the years his job had become more and more physically demanding and after ten years of faithful service he found himself looking for other employment. In November of 1991 he began a new career with a company that would provide not only a better salary but much better benefits including educational benefits and within the year Rhonnie returned to school part-time to pursue his degree in accounting.

Christopher celebrated his 11th birthday in the spring of 1992, another year that began uneventfully but is remembered for a couple of remarkable reasons, and though he and I remained close I could sense a slight pulling away as he completed the 4th grade that spring. He had been blessed that year with an outstanding Christian teacher who had not only been a first-rate teacher but also very loving and supportive as well. Christopher had also become very good friends with another 4th grade boy whose mother was also a teacher and the two of them seemed to have a friendly competition with one another to see who could get the better grades. It had been a great year and Christopher had received excellent grades and we were very, very proud of the young man he was becoming.

Sandi was homeschooling her daughter and I had been increasingly and inexplicably drawn to the idea even though I still didn't feel in the least bit equipped or qualified to do the same for Christopher. Quite honestly though, I had been becoming more and more interested in, or perhaps I should say fascinated with the notion of homeschooling, because it suddenly seemed that more and more people at our church were teaching their own children.

I was also becoming increasingly disturbed by the trend to take all Christian values and teaching out of the public school system while allowing other religions and ungodly values to subtly infiltrate. I suppose it would be accurate to say in retrospect that I felt that we were being drawn to look into the idea of homeschooling Christopher but when I'd mentioned the subject to Rhonnie about a year earlier he'd been adamant that we would not be doing any such thing. We rationalized that everyone we knew that homeschooled their children were either extremely brilliant, extremely brave, extremely crazy or all the above!

Besides, we had yet to see how any of the kids would actually turn out. The entire idea was, for the most part dismissed except for the fact that when the Lord is the one who has planted the idea in the first place it has a way of hanging on; why else would there suddenly be so many homeschooling families at New Life Center when a few years earlier the idea had been nearly unheard of?

Soon a series of events would change our hearts and our minds about homeschooling. First, over that summer Christopher began to grow up at an alarming rate; in many ways he'd always seemed more mature than many of his peers and for reasons I can't even begin to explain I found I was dreading sending him back to school in the fall. During an August trip to Disney World Christopher had announced to me, during the fireworks display at the Epcot Center of all places, that he didn't want to grow up. We'd been having a last summer fling, just the two of us, before he returned to school in a few days and the announcement not only stunned me, it broke my heart, because I'd felt he was growing up far too quickly and I also knew from my own experience how quickly the innocence of childhood can disappear. We left the Epcot Center that evening arm in arm and with tears streaming down both our faces as I told him that he needn't be in too big a hurry yet knowing that he would grow up all too soon. We returned from that trip the very day that school began and the next day our son officially became a 5th grader.

For some reason there had not been any boys Christopher's age at New Life Center for a couple of years so our son had become friendly with some really nice boys that were about two years older and because of that we had arranged with our Youth Pastor (a very understanding youth pastor I might add) to allow him to promote into the youth group a year early. A highly anticipated move I might add, especially for someone who a few weeks earlier had expressed a desire to not grow up. He was immediately accepted in the youth group attending every service, afterglow and youth function that could possibly be managed. In October Christopher attended the annual youth convention in Oklahoma City. He had a great time and in addition to his physical and emotional growth we were awestruck by his spiritual growth as well. He was thriving and I had all but put the notion of homeschooling completely out of my mind.

About two weeks after the convention Christopher very suddenly became ill and because he was running a slight fever and complaining of fatigue and a few aches and pains he missed a couple of days of school. Within a few days he seemed to be as good as new so we sent him to school only to have him sent home before the day was over feeling ill again and running a slight fever. This scenario was repeated several times over the next few weeks and in early November, realizing that this was not an ailment that would subside on its own, we took our son to the doctor and after ruling everything else out Christopher was diagnosed with the Epstein-Barr virus. Incidentally, two girls in the youth group were also diagnosed with the same ailment around the same time. Turns out they'd all three shared a large soft drink while at the convention!

After doing some research and talking to others I learned a couple of things about Epstein-Barr that I would like not to have known. First, it can be unpredictable and must run its course (at least that was the case in 1992). Its unpredictability certainly presented itself in our son's case in that we never knew from one day to the next whether he would be well enough to go to school or not. If he went, we didn't know if he'd be able to stay. I doubt he attended school an entire week the remainder of that semester. Once I was even letting him out of the car when he informed me that he didn't feel like he could make it so we turned right around and went back home and he slept the rest of the day.

The other and more disturbing fact I learned about Epstein-Barr was that it was associated with Chronic Fatigue Syndrome and I had recently become acquainted with a lady with CFS who had been sick, and getting sicker, I might add, for years. Not only is Epstein-Barr unpredictable, it runs its course at different rates for different individuals. This woman had become so ill over the years that there were days on end that she couldn't get out of bed. I just couldn't imagine that this is what my 11 year old had to look forward to or the two girls from church, for that matter.

By Christmastime we had come to the realization that our son had missed almost as much school as he had attended that fall and at the suggestion of the school a home-bound teacher was arranged who would come to our home once a week to bring classroom assignments for the following week and review lessons from the past week. It seemed like a good solution. The stress of wondering if our son would make it to school or not would be eliminated and we could concentrate on getting him well. We began the home-bound program in January of 1993 with the beginning of the spring semester. Because I felt the responsibility for overseeing the school work throughout the week in addition to providing occasional help I would sit at the table with Christopher and the teacher as lessons were reviewed and assignments were given.

We had been with the home-bound program approximately three weeks when I received a most startling and completely unexpected revelation. One day I had to show the teacher the millimeters on the ruler we were using and actually had to explain to her the difference between millimeters and centimeters. (The mm that appears next to the markings is something of a clue.) I'm not sure that when she left our house that day she was entirely convinced of what I was showing her but at least she had given Christopher credit for answering a problem correctly and she would not have done so otherwise. I felt as though God had spoken directly to me through the incident (I had already been feeling an increasing sense that perhaps I might have to consider approaching Rhonnie about rethinking homeschooling for our son). As I prayed over our situation and for Christopher's healing I definitely began to feel that perhaps the Lord had allowed this illness into our sons life for the purpose of our realizing that He in fact had been calling us to homeschool and that the time to do so was now.

    I also began to realize when I prayed that I had deliberately tuned out the voice of the Lord a year earlier when the idea of homeschooling had first been introduced. When my husband had said "no" I gave up (and yes I admit that I did so with a sigh of relief). I should have asked the Lord to change Rhonnie's heart as well as to confirm what I thought I might be hearing and I should have asked Him to open the door for us to do what He was calling us to but I chose to dismiss it taking the easy way out. Would our son still have gotten sick if I had listened and obeyed? Only the Lord knows that but what I knew the day of the ruler incident was that I could teach my child and that I probably could do it very well with the right support and resources and those had certainly already been provided in abundance; by now our church had a very active support group for homeschooling families. So, the Ramirez's joined the ranks of New Life Centers extremely brilliant, extremely brave and extremely crazy; we were also extremely overwhelmed yet confident too that we had heard from God and we knew we were doing the right thing.

    We finished the spring semester of 5th grade with flying colors and we all breathed a huge sigh of relief. Christopher had celebrated his 12th birthday in April and when it came time to make the decision whether or not to allow him to go to youth camp Rhonnie and I really struggled because though Christopher's physical condition had improved considerably he was far from well. There were still days he felt achy, feverish and tired and as it had been from the beginning, those days were completely unpredictable. Having been to camp myself I knew that the pace could be grueling for a healthy person and we envisioned sending our son to camp on Monday, then being called to come and get him on Tuesday. (Sound familiar?) Of course, he wanted to go to camp very badly and was by now a solid member of the Cutting Edge, New Life Center's youth group and we knew he was being blessed by being a part of this group. In the end we sent him to camp and agreed to trust God for the outcome and while our son was attending camp he received complete and forever healing of any and all traces of the Epstein-Barr virus!

We of course, knew, healed or not, we were committed to homeschooling for the duration and we knew the Lord had directed us to do so and though the next years were rewarding they also proved to be very challenging in some ways. I continued to work at Saint Francis part time and Rhonnie was now a part time college student, we remained the children's church leaders and as a way to juggle all his responsibilities Rhonnie was working nights on a fulltime basis. I'm amazed looking back that he actually found a way to work, attend classes (six to nine hours a semester), study, share in the homeschooling and go to church regularly. Many a Saturday my husband has worked all night long, come home to change clothes and then teach a Sunday school class, play his violin during worship and actually stay (mostly) awake for the church service!

Actually, though the schedule we kept during those few years sounds quite nightmarish, it turned out to be a very good situation for Rhonnie and Christopher. They certainly had more time one on one than they would have had if Christopher had been in a school room all day long.

I would have pulled my hair out by the roots if Rhonnie had not agreed to teach our son math so we were able to arrange our schedules so that Rhonnie would oversee the homeschooling while I worked and on my days off I would teach the subjects I enjoyed; science, English and writing projects. The greater challenge was to find time that Rhonnie and I could spend together when we weren't both exhausted. Another challenge we faced was that our son had experienced just enough of public school that after he was well he wanted to return there. That was not an option and though he occasionally grumbled his attitude remained very good for the most part.

As Christopher entered adolescence I felt as though the Lord was leading me to stay as involved as I could in his life. I was certain that part of the reason we were homeschooling had to do with His plan for Christopher but I didn't realize for a very long time that it had just as much to do with His plan for me. At some point we had transitioned from God's Gang to teaching the junior high Sunday school class. We had made that transition the year that our son moved on to the senior high class. Soon an opportunity presented itself that I had long thought would be the most exciting area of ministry in the church; and we responded to a plea for youth sponsors. I loved being involved in youth ministry and once again I gave myself wholeheartedly to what I had been called to for a season by going to camp for several summers and attending most every youth rally, function and outing that I could.

Rhonnie and I were youth sponsors through several fine youth pastors over a period of about six years. I learned to minister to others in a different way during this season of my life. For one thing I really identified with many of the situations and circumstances the young people faced. Teenagers today face very real challenges in serving the Lord because the opportunities for sin are so much more prevalent than they were in my day. I also believe that today's young people face many things that the average teenager was not often confronted with when I was a teenager in the 60's.

It isn't so much that there are new areas of sin to explore but our society has made sin more appealing, accessible and acceptable. When I was in high school about the worst thing you could do in public was to smoke a cigarette in the bathroom between classes yet the very ones who frowned upon that behavior at school were smoking in their cars or in their bedrooms. The same was true with sexual activity. I believe that the number of sexually active young people was a lot higher than I imagined as a teen and I knew a few that engaged in it. But if one was caught she became the talk of the school; today having babies out of wedlock has become almost a status symbol for some. In addition to these concerns and the resulting consequences, we have to worry about our teenagers using drugs that can kill them or alter their minds forever, among other things.

During our years as youth sponsors I not only felt for the first time that I had found a group of people to minister to that I could truly identify with, I found that even the kids who seemed to have everything; godly parents, good grades, friends and a comfortable home faced challenges that I'd never dreamed of. I believe my Father was bringing me through my teenage years again by allowing me to see those years in a different perspective. Not only was I now able to be the voice to so many young people that I had not heard in my teenage years, I was also able to see that even those who seemed to be the most together often felt awkward, lonely, different and even invisible, just as I had once felt.

I also began to see that there were many young people who faced difficulties that I hadn't even imagined; like the absolute horror of physical and sexual abuse, real financial hardships, bullies at school and parents that just didn't seem to care about them at all. I got to know several very young women who were committed to follow Jesus yet their parents cared nothing about God or godliness. These girls were practically raising themselves, caring for siblings and even their parents from time to time! We opened our home to one such young woman for several months when her situation at home became unbearable.

As a result of homeschooling, Christopher was able to participate in Praisong, a traveling music ministry, two years earlier than he would have been allowed to had he remained in public school and he was also able to graduate and go to college two years ahead of his peers; something I don't necessarily recommend and I certainly wasn't ready for it but in August of 1998 Rhonnie and I took our seventeen year old son to Southwestern Assemblies of God University in Waxahachie, Texas. I don't think we looked at each other once on our drive home after leaving him there; I know I was crying and I'm pretty sure Rhonnie shed a tear or two as well. I know that I was in no way ready for an empty nest and I wasn't entirely sure how we were going to handle our new status in life. For the next few months I worked as many hours as I could and though there was no longer any reason to do so, I missed every single lady's meeting at New Life Center, as I had for the last couple of years while focusing on the youth ministry.

We remained active as youth sponsors and I continued to find involvement in that area very rewarding as well as a way to stay connected to young people now that we no longer had one in our home. By now I had all but abandoned my dream to minister to women. I had immersed myself instead into being a mother, by involving myself in youth ministry and teaching first Junior high then high school Sunday school classes. Yes, God was bringing me up in the way I should have grown up as first a child, then a young person, teaching me at every level fundamental truths and building my inner person just as a parent would raise a child up in the way he should go.

I look back on those years as some of the best years of my life, at least up until now, and I see them in absolute awe now that I realize what the Lord was doing for me during that time. I'd said all along that I functioned at more or less the same level as a teenager but our days in youth ministry were numbered and over the next year I would find that I still had a bit more growing up to do.

Jennifer was now married and we became instant Grammy and Grampy to the little bonus boy that came with her sweet husband. By the end of the decade we had three grandsons! Along with the fun and anticipated changes that come with a growing family we had to face the untimely death of Rhonnie's mother; one of the most Christ-like people I've ever known. In the meantime, Christopher thrived at Southwestern, he had a great roommate and auditioned for and was accepted into one of the school's vocal groups, the Chorale.

We now absolutely lived for opportunities to see our son, either through his visits home or our visits there and neither seemed to be frequent enough. In early November we took my mother to Waxahachie to a concert presented by the Chorale and she was overjoyed to see her grandson doing so well. She was extremely proud of him.

My mother had always been in relatively good health though she had neglected herself terribly since her retirement. She had developed some poor eating habits and that along with inactivity had caused her to gain a great deal of weight. She had complained about various issues to her physician but he never seemed to be able to find anything wrong with her and though she continued to take medication for depression he pronounced her in good health. That weekend would be a very memorable one for two reasons.

After attending the concert on Friday evening we were introduced to Erica, the girl who we all just knew would be our future daughter-in-law. There was a lot of activity that evening, and of course after the concert, we all went out to eat with a car load of our son's friends before heading to our hotel. After a very long day my mother was exhausted and so were we.

On Saturday, we had determined to tackle the Grapevine Mills Mall, not a small undertaking for the sturdiest of individuals yet it was something that my mother could easily have done a few months earlier. We both loved to shop and had planned to do some substantial Christmas shopping that day. As we shopped my mother seemed to tire more quickly than I had ever seen her tire; at one point during the day she had to stop in her tracks and lean against a wall to catch her breath. When I looked at her I was alarmed by what I saw; her face was bright red, she was perspiring heavily and she was noticeably distressed but after a few seconds she insisted she was able to continue on. After stopping for a rest and a snack she seemed herself again though we did cut our shopping trip short. We didn't leave her at her doorstep the next day until she promised to call her doctor first thing Monday morning.

For the next few months my mother continued to receive a clean bill of health though she repeatedly said that she didn't feel well; in the end we both attributed her situation to getting older and being overweight. During this time I was battling my own health issues and in December, after struggling with whether or not to have a recommended hysterectomy I decided that I would take the plunge if for no other reason than the improved quality of life that would surely ensue. I had fiercely resisted the notion and now I'm not sure why except in the back of my mind was the idea that I could still have another baby. I was by now fifty years old but I wanted to hold out for menopause never wanting to stay the hand of God again. But I had suffered quite a lot over the years with uterine fibroids and after literally years of prayer and weighing all the pros and cons my physician scheduled me for a complete hysterectomy to be done in late January, 1999.

Meanwhile, my mother had not felt able to make the trip to our house for Christmas so we had taken Christmas to her and I realized I would have to visit her much more frequently though her condition never seemed to really change much from one visit to the next. Gratefully, she had wonderful neighbors who looked in on her and provided food while I recovered from my surgery. Consequently several weeks went by before I would see her again in March. By then my mother had declined considerably and I knew I would have to be much more attentive to her needs and to be quite honest I felt like a duck out of water. Five years earlier I had begged her to consider making a move to the Tulsa area but she had refused so I envisioned weekly trips to Oklahoma City for the next however many years she had left. I worked at least forty hours every week, drove to Oklahoma City on Friday, back home on Sunday only to do it all over again the next weekend.

In mid-May I varied only slightly from that routine the week that Christopher came home from Southwestern for the summer. I went out to dinner and a movie with all three of my children and had one of the most outstanding times with the three of them that I can ever remember having. The next day I went to Oklahoma City bright and early to do the usual; clean my mother's apartment, do her laundry, shop for groceries and see if there would be anything else I could do for her until the next weekend. The minute I walked in the door I could see that her situation had worsened considerately over that past week. She was weak, she hadn't eaten, the neighbors were worried and I knew that I would not be able to leave her alone for another week. I was also quite concerned over the fact that even though my mother was now noticeably sicker by the day her doctor still could find nothing wrong with her! I knew she was truly ill when she offered no resistance to my announcement that I would not be returning home without her.

Our drive from Oklahoma City to Broken Arrow that Sunday was uneventful if not actually pleasant. Of course, I was wondering how in the world I would manage to work, take care of my mother and keep my sanity. It seems I'd transitioned very nicely from having once worried about how I would handle an empty nest to absolutely loving a quiet, peaceful house. About ten years earlier my mother had decided that she actually liked me. She apparently also discovered that she really liked talking to me because that is exactly what she did whenever we were together. She would talk non-stop, often following me from one room to the next as she carried on (an often one-sided) conversation and I wasn't sure how I would handle that day in and day out.

Her apartment had been on the second floor and until that last week she had been going regularly to the mail box so we determined that she would do just fine in one of our upstairs bedrooms. Only our master bedroom was downstairs and she wouldn't hear of our giving it up for her. She was exhausted from the trip but did indeed get up the stairs easily enough. On Monday I went to work while Rhonnie and Christopher stayed at home with her but when I returned home that day my mother was in such distress that she couldn't catch her breath. I immediately put her in the car and took her to the Saint Francis emergency room.

It seems that we waited the compulsory eternity in the small curtained room before even seeing a physician who ordered, among other things, a complete blood count. After the blood was drawn we waited another eternity for the results and when they came we were shocked. My mother had continued to suspect that she might be diabetic, though her doctor had repeatedly said she was not, and even though she had not been diagnosed with any other malady we both knew that something was wrong and now we just wanted to know what that might be so she could be properly treated.

Neither of us ever considered that she might have leukemia and when the doctor did come in to reveal that the lab indicated her white blood cells were off the charts we were stunned but also a bit relieved that we at least now knew what she was facing. Within the hour my mother was admitted to the hospital and by the next day she had seen an oncologist and had received her first chemotherapy. The doctor assured us that her prognosis was very, very good and that she would likely even be able to live on her own again and she and I agreed that when she was able her home would be in Broken Arrow or Tulsa this time, not Oklahoma City.

Through June and July my mother continued to stay with us but now, because the stairs had become just too much for her, she occupied a corner of the living room, sleeping in her favorite old green arm chair, one she had slept in for years because she had not liked sleeping in either of the bedrooms in her apartment. She made regular visits to the oncologist, received prescribed chemotherapy treatments and for every one step forward it seemed that she took two or even three steps backwards. She really seemed to make no progress at all. Not only was she not feeling any better her regular lab work indicated that her white blood cells were not diminishing as they should.

By early August she was forced to make a decision as to whether or not the chemotherapy should be increased. I still have mixed feelings regarding the decision that was made and am not at all sure how I might decide if I ever have to face making the decision for myself. In the end we chose to go for the more aggressive chemotherapy in hopes that some real improvement would be made. I am not one to ever give up hope. "I wait for the Lord, my soul does wait, and in His word do I hope. My soul waits for the Lord more than the watchmen for the morning; *indeed, more than* the watchmen for the morning. O Israel, hope in the Lord for with the Lord there is lovingkindness, and with Him is abundant redemption. And He will redeem Israel from all his iniquities." (Psalm 130:5-8). In my mother's case I was hoping for so much more than mere physical healing.

The first week of August in 1999 my mother took her first and only more aggressive treatment of chemotherapy. By the end of that week she was once again in Saint Francis Hospital, so sick and so weak that she could not raise her head from her pillow, in fact she seemed oblivious even to where she was or who was there with her. She had tubes everywhere and the doctor was now telling us that not only would there be no more chemotherapy, it was unlikely my mother would go home from the hospital.

Prayer warriors were summoned as the family gathered and slowly and miraculously my mother got stronger and began to communicate with us again. Three weeks later she came home, this time with a hospital bed to replace the old green chair and a team of wonderful caregivers from Saint Francis Hospice. It truly was a miracle and I felt that it was a second opportunity my dear Father had given my mother to live a few more months and to have every opportunity to come to know Him. "The Lord is not slow about His promise, as some count slowness, but is patient toward you, not wishing for any to perish but for all to come to repentance." (2 Peter 3:9). It would also prove to be an incredible opportunity for me to see something in my mother that I would never have seen otherwise and for Rhonnie and me to truly live our lives before her showing her the love of God as we continued to pray for her healing and her salvation.

My mother returned to our home on a hot August Saturday. On the Friday before I had left my job at Saint Francis behind telling my wonderful boss and the sweet people that I worked with that it would be a leave of absence but I knew in my heart that I would never return there and I knew I would never regret that decision. There was of course, nothing that could be done medically for my mother but I knew that she would need someone with her to see to her needs throughout the day. The hospice team visited regularly and we all found every one of them delightful. We looked forward to their visits and I was pleasantly surprised to find that the majority of those who visited from hospice had strong faith and real working relationships with the Lord. They prayed with her and with me for her. My mother began regularly reading Christopher's Adventure Bible, the one she'd given him years earlier, and we even talked about the Lord on occasion but she remained reserved and at least verbally, noncommittal on a personal level.

One of the things that began to really amaze me was my mother's attitude. She was downright cheerful, pleasant and lovable; she was finally completely Naomi! The old Mara was gone and I realized she had been steadily disappearing over the last several years. I'd just had difficulty recognizing Naomi because I'd known Mara all too well. It had been Mara I'd always related to, feared and even hated at times. It had been Mara around whom I'd always had to maintain my guard. I wasn't always sure how to relate to this woman who even though she was dying a little each day seemed always to think more of us than of herself. She began each day with a cheery 'good morning' and wore a smile throughout each day. I determined that though there had been many things about my mother that I refused to emulate that this grace in the face of catastrophic illness and certain death would not be one of them. I pray that if I am ever in that position that I might behave with the same grace and dignity that she displayed in her last months. My Father provided for me a role model in Naomi that Mara could never have been.

On October 31, 1999, an absolutely beautiful fall day, a remarkable thing happened and truly the day will be one that I will always remember fondly. One of the first things my mother had done when she knew that she would be moving in to our home was to arrange to have a housekeeping service come once a week to do some basic cleaning and to take some of the burden of running the home off my shoulders. I really appreciated it and enjoyed the extravagance of it all. On rare occasions we would try to leave the house when they came but more often than not my mother was too ill even to dress so the ladies worked around us. On this day though, my mother said that she thought she might like to get out of the house for awhile and knowing the cleaning ladies were coming we ventured out for a drive.

First we picked up lunch at a drive-through and then went in search of fall color. We managed to get lost (in Broken Arrow, no less) and ended up in Coweta which had not been our original destination. Then we decided we needed some pecans. My mother loved pecans and could eat them until she was almost sick and since every fall I try to pick up five or ten pounds for the holidays we took the long way to Bixby where we stocked up.

By the time we returned home we'd been gone for several hours and still my mother wasn't tired so we sat at the table and divided our pecans into several smaller portions for the freezer, eating a handful here and there. We'd laughed a lot that day and at the end of the day we began to actually make plans for what we would do the next day and even the next week. Beautiful fall days will from now on remind me of the fun we had just being together that day; a day that I believe was another gift to me from my Father; an experience with my mother that I would always cherish. Don't you know that when He thinks about His children, as He does continually, He's also thinking of creative ways to bless us and fulfill the desires of our hearts?

The next day though, my mother could barely get out of bed again and there would not be another outing for us. We would have forty-six more days together. During that time we shopped for Christmas, ordering from catalogs and from one of the television shopping channels, ate whatever we wanted, worked jigsaw and crossword puzzles and spent as much time with my children and grandchildren as possible. They were good days and peaceful days in our home. If it was possible to do so, I found a new appreciation for my husband in that he never seemed stressed or burdened by my mother's presence in our home and he dealt with my stress so lovingly that even she noticed and told me often how truly wonderful he is. The hospice nurses would often comment about the peaceful atmosphere in our home and I never missed an opportunity to give God the glory for that. I'm amazed at that wonderful presence even now.

My mother celebrated her eighty-fifth birthday on December 15th with Andy and Jennifer and Jennifer's family gathered around. That night as she was taking a drink of water she was noticeably weaker and had slept more than usual that day. I slept on the sofa that was just a few feet from her bed that night. The next day she didn't wake up but remained in a deep sleep and when the nurse arrived midmorning she began to talk with me about what I already knew in my heart. My mother would not be with us much longer and would likely not even make it through the night. I thought of all the thoughtfully purchased gifts that lay under the tree. Gifts that she would have preferred to have given as soon as they'd arrived but in an attempt to give her something to look forward to I'd persuaded her to wait until Christmas morning. Now she wouldn't see

Rhonnie's reaction to the whimsical Padre that serves as a birdfeeder on our patio or Jennifer's reaction to the three bean bag chairs, each with beautifully embroidered names for her boys.

I had begun to pray that day before my feet touched the floor and I began to get a sense that there was something very important and very personal going on in that room. I truly believe that in keeping with everything I know to be true about my Father's grace, mercy and love for His creation that in His desire that none should perish He gives one opportunity after another for repentance and acceptance of His love and forgiveness until we draw our very last breath. His presence was powerful that day and I felt that even as my mother lay dying that the Lord was answering my prayers and that He was ministering to her in a way that no one else ever could.

On a couple of occasions I even felt His presence so strongly that I didn't approach her bed because I felt that in doing so I might interfere with the work that the Lord Himself was doing. I had a strange peace; strange in light of the fact that in the natural sense I had no idea what my mother believed - she'd embraced Catholicism for a time as a young woman and had later professed to an atheist - but in the supernatural sense I knew that the Lord Jesus was not only ministering to her but to me as well. I was acutely aware that "...but with God all things are possible." (Matthew 19:26).

At 10:30 p.m. on December 16, 1999 my mother passed into His arms and my life and my world would be forever changed again. There would be yet another platform for ministry as I dealt with grief that in years past I would not have imagined possible. And my Fathers thoughts toward this daughter would continue to outnumber the sand.

Chapter Nine
His Enemies and Mine

"O that You would slay the wicked, O God; Depart from me, therefore, men of bloodshed. Do I not hate those who hate You, O LORD? And do I not loathe those who rise up against You? I hate them with the utmost hatred; they have become my enemies." (Psalm 139:19-22)

I am so glad I realized my mother wasn't my enemy long before she passed away. At the beginning of this story I said that my mother's story was an integral part of my own and her influence certainly has had a profound effect on me throughout my life. Indeed, I did many things my mother would never have thought of doing in my efforts to distance myself from what I perceived her to be. Our relationship wasn't at all enhanced by my declaration that I intended to do everything possible to ensure I would be nothing like her when I grew up.

For more years than I can recall our relationship suffered significantly due to choices I made in pursuit of that goal. Furthermore, for so long she seemed as unable (or unwilling) to let go of our past as she had been to let go of the history she'd shared with her mother and brother. Even after Rhonnie and I had been married for many years she would astound me with an occasional criticism or comment that was completely without merit. She continued to surprise me with her imaginary observations even after I'd determined to follow the Lord and after I believed she had acknowledged that my marriage to Rhonnie was good.

It was only a few years before my mother passed away that I began to see real changes in her attitude toward me. When, as a teenager I began to sense a lack of support and understanding in almost everything I undertook I'd stopped confiding in her. Many years later that lack of support was still evident, especially during the years Rhonnie and I tried to have another child. She showed no compassion or empathy for our plight even expressing her aversion to the very idea of it on the rare occasion that the subject came up.

The first indication I had that my mother's heart might be softening came when we made the decision to homeschool Christopher. Even knowing we'd made a God directed decision I had dreaded telling my mother and I'd armed myself with every bit of positive information and our own concrete plans before broaching the subject. To my complete surprise she embraced the idea with open arms. She completely understood that Christopher's physical condition prevented him from regularly attending school and she'd not only been concerned about his health, she'd worried he would fall behind in school. I was pleasantly surprised by her support and even more so by the fact that her support and encouragement never declined.

Though still sometimes shaky, my mother and I had finally found common ground in my children; her precious grandchildren that she was so proud of. I loved sharing their accomplishments with her and I continue to realize how much I miss her when one of my children or grandchildren has news to share. How I would have loved for her to see Christopher marry, she'd loved Erica from the very first meeting, graduate from college and introduce her to Christopher's son; I know she would have fallen head over heels in love! She'd be so proud of Andy and Jennifer and Jennifer's boys as well.

During her last few years my mother actually began to tell me she was proud of me on occasion. Sadly, I was having some trouble adjusting to her new attitude because it was such a departure from the mother I had known; as a result I didn't always know how to respond to her. However, she remained hard hearted when our conversations turned to the Lord and in many ways her changed attitude that should have brought us closer only seemed to emphasis the deep spiritual chasm that existed between us. I love to talk about the Lord, His ways, His Word and all I continue to learn about Him; He's my favorite subject! I love to tell others of the ways He continues to bless me and work in my life but, for the most part, those subjects remained off limits with my mother.

Nevertheless, I am so thankful for the opportunity God gave me to identify my mother's enemies as a means of dealing with the fiery darts that Satan sends my way on occasion. I'm also thankful that during my mother's last months my Father showed me that there were, in fact, many things about my mother that I could appreciate and embrace. I will always credit her for my love of animals and music and I am so glad she introduced me to the things she loved by taking me to concerts, art galleries and on vacations. I no longer fear that I might become her having learned to reject only those things about her that would displease my Father if I held on to them. In fact as the twentieth century came to a close I was just beginning to identify my own true enemy and I finally realized that fear and anger were only weapons that he'd aimed at unprotected areas of my heart in much the same way he'd used those weapons against my mother.

Fear had been one of my mother's worst enemies and as she aged her fears became more and more intensified. Fear was something of a driving force in my mother's life and it often kept her from normal, everyday activities; like going to a shopping mall, even during the day and she rarely went out at night and never, ever alone. She feared her purse would be snatched or her car would be hijacked. She feared someone would break into her apartment and assault her. She feared she might run out of money and end up on the street. And we just didn't want to tell her if we were planning to travel in an airplane!

Furthermore, those fears were often triggered by the evening news but my mother, who was an avid reader of all kinds of books, especially loved ghost stories and she would often read until the wee hours of the morning. In addition to being extremely fearful she also had complained for years that she didn't sleep well at night. Is it any wonder why? Through the years my mother had become a product of everything she allowed into her mind and in addition, for years her closest friend was an agoraphobic who lived in the apartment next door. This woman was so fearful of going out that she actually died alone in her living room rather than call for help when she knew she was having a heart attack! I can't imagine that the two of them were even remotely good for one another.

I'd learned from my brief stint as a single mother that I simply could not read a scary book or watch a horror movie if I was going to live alone with my children. I had been very fearful of the dark as a child and I realized I needed to overcome my fear of being alone at night if we were going to survive. I knew I didn't want to teach fear for fears sake to my children. In the end this had nothing to do with godly principle only with self (and sanity) preservation, besides, reality was frightening enough in those days.

Anger is another of Satan's favorite weapons because anger not only destroys the one who is angry but handled correctly (at least by his standards) anger can be used to destroy innocent lives, marriages, and even total strangers when taken to the extreme. Anger was an even greater stronghold for my mother than fear. Exactly the way an underlying spirit of anger had been for me for a time! She had the ability to become absolutely furious and many times when I observed her fury as a young child I wasn't entirely sure at whom it was directed. Her outbursts frightened me occasionally when I was little but I later learned to respond to her anger with equal wrath.

I'd developed a pattern of internalizing my feelings, so as not to provoke her until I just couldn't hold them in any longer. Then, I would overreact with all sorts of outrage. I believe we call those displays temper tantrums and I was oh, so good at them. Temper tantrums actually worked on my mother; at least they worked some of the time, but when a temper tantrum didn't work I usually ended up with even more bottled up emotion and more internalized anger. Anger is a formidable and destructive enemy of God to be sure.

For the most part my own anger reached its peak during my marriage to Carl, who was also a very angry person. Carl and I never learned to communicate with one another and I often had difficulty expressing myself so I would become not only angry with myself but with him as well only the temper tantrum never worked with Carl. In that last year of marriage many an argument ended with one of us throwing something at the other and I truly believe that if the marriage had continued we would have eventually become physically violent with one another.

It actually took me quite some time to adjust to living with someone who wasn't angry all the time when I married Rhonnie. God surely provided an example of gentleness in my sweet husband. Even during our most difficult early years he never raised his voice and never wanted to argue and since he began serving the Lord he has never seemed discouraged or particularly stressed. Yet disappointment and ensuing discouragement were two huge anger inducers in me and I was often discouraged, frustrated and angry enough for both of us. When my mother became ill and moved into our home thankfully, anger was not the issue for either of us it once had been.

Nevertheless for more years than I care to acknowledge anger was a habit and a way of life for me and became my natural reaction to just about everything that presented as a problem to me. When there wasn't enough money or enough family time I was angry or completely non-communicative. When I didn't get my way I would sulk and I did so, well into my forties when I should have known better and in fact, did know better but old habits are often very difficult to break. The Bible has a lot to say about anger but I often had great difficulty applying scriptural principles to my life in this area. (I'd also learned to conveniently blame hormones for much of my irritability.) "Let all bitterness and wrath and anger and clamor and slander be put away from you, along with all malice." (Ephesians 4:31). "But now you also, put them all aside: anger, wrath, malice, slander, and abusive speech from your mouth." (Colossians 3:8).

It would take a specific word from the Lord, via Rhonnie, before I would begin to deal with irritability and anger once and for all. Certainly, my mother did bring out a lot of the worst in me as did stress, fatigue and any life circumstance that might have been unwelcome or unexpected but many times I didn't need a reason to be angry or irritable; I just was. I believe now, that a lot of my mother's anger was directed at everyone or no one but most likely it was probably just directed at herself. Once, after my mother had visited our home for a weekend I complained to Rhonnie about something she had said or done. I'll never forget his response "Sometimes you act just like she does", he'd said. That was a very unwelcome wake-up call and I knew I'd have to deal with that spirit of anger if I was to achieve my goal of becoming more Christ-like. That had long ago replaced my original goal of not becoming my mother and I realized that day that I wasn't as close to achieving either as I would have liked.

Back in 1980 when I fully committed my life to the Lord I acquired an instant aversion to many of the enemies of God that had bound me in the past; at least the tangible sins, like immorality. I soon realized that if I was going to serve Him completely I would not be able to drink at all anymore and that was fine with me. What I didn't realize at the time was that I had not even begun to identify my truest enemies. I now know that there is really only one enemy, the one identified in scripture as Satan, but he likes to present himself in many different disguises and fear, anger and immorality are just three on a very long list of sins God's Word instructs us to avoid because these sins are so deadly and destructive.

"The thief comes only to steal and kill and destroy; I came that they may have life, and have it abundantly." (John 10:10). Satan's mission is to steal, kill and destroy God's people and he will attempt to accomplish it anyway he can. His plan for our lives differs greatly from God's in that his plan is not tailor made for us; rather, he just tries every weapon in his evil arsenal until he finds something that happens to work. I don't believe he is at all privy to God's personalized, fearful and wonderful plan for every individual He creates but our enemy knows human nature and he knows the scriptures and that God's plan is for "welfare ... that we may have a future and a hope." (Jeremiah 29:11). Satan will gleefully do whatever he can to introduce calamity, rob us of our future and leave us completely without hope and that is what makes him such an insidious and dangerous enemy!

I remember very well the last scary movie I watched and the resulting nightmare that ensued and this was after Rhonnie and I were married and after I had rededicated my life to the Lord; when I thought very erroneously that I could handle such things again. This movie was based on a very popular novel and had been highly touted and anticipated; that is probably why I allowed myself to see it. I related to this particular movie in a whole new way and in it I believe I saw a manifestation of real evil. For weeks I could hardly close my eyes without seeing that manifestation all over again and I couldn't help wondering what kind of warped imagination could conceive such a story! Apparently I also had acquired an aversion to horror movies and I knew that I would not indulge in such God-dishonoring and fear producing 'entertainment' again.

I also began to realize that I had a real aversion to bad language and sex in movies and as Christopher grew older I also realized that I just didn't enjoy even most movies with a PG-13 rating; even a few of the PG movies I've seen lately have crossed a line. I prefer not to see movies that contain material or language my children and grandchildren can't watch even when they aren't present; it's become kind of a family joke. Why? Because, I recognize something that my mother did not; we are very much a product of what we feed into our minds whether it is fear, immorality or anger that is produced.

I even found certain popular music that I had previously enjoyed would occasionally make me almost physically ill, especially certain songs that would almost instantly transport me back to a time, place or activity that I was now so ashamed to have been involved in. I believe that 2 Corinthians 10:3-5 gives a great deal of insight not only into the enemy of God but how we can most effectively deal with him, particularly in regard to our imaginations. "For though we walk in the flesh, we do not war according to the flesh, for the weapons of our warfare are not of the flesh, but divinely powerful for the destruction of fortresses. We are destroying speculations and every lofty thing raised up against the knowledge of God, and we are taking every thought captive to the obedience of Christ…" Sin, begins with a thought that has been introduced by God's enemy, and when thoughts are not taken captive they soon rise up against God! Thank God He has equipped us with divinely powerful weapons for their destruction.

In fact, it is bad language that brought one of the most blatant attacks I ever received from the enemy, and again, it was the direct result of a movie I had seen. Except during those times that my husband has worked nights or evenings we have always gotten up very early. Often he must be at work by six o'clock and as a result I discovered some time ago that I am a lot more productive in the mornings than at any other time of day. I also firmly believe that morning time is the very best time of day to have devotions and to spend time with the Lord; whether it's six or eight a.m., the first hours of my day are generally spent with the Lord; once I get involved with other daily activities its all over for me.

One morning I was praying on our front porch, when seemingly out of nowhere I began to be absolutely assaulted by a word; a four letter word that makes me very angry when I hear it and no matter how I tried to drown out the word it seems that every time I let my guard down for a moment the word would come back into my thoughts even to the point that I was not completely sure I had not uttered it, though I knew I had not. Over the next several days it seemed I could not go to prayer without that word eventually entering into my thoughts. I recognized this as a true expression of the enemy's hatred of God and if he was trying to prevent me from praying he was beginning to succeed.

As I began to earnestly seek God He brought to my attention the last PG-13 movie I'd seen and I had enjoyed it up until the language unexpectedly and unnecessarily assaulted the poor audience. This particular movie had been highly anticipated, an adventure movie with a favorite actor, thankfully at least, he wasn't the one that had spoken the word. Because this one word stirred up such anger in me I feared for a very long while after that incident that I might utter the word myself. "...For the mouth speaks out of that which fills the heart." (Matthew 12:34). So, what is the most recent movie I've seen? *Cars*, thank you very much, and I thoroughly, thoroughly enjoyed it. One of the best ways I have found to deal with the enemy is to restrict his access to my mind by making every effort not to feed on anything that he might feed on later.

The one area that I can say with any certainty I had dealt with early on is bitterness and that had been vanquished when I participated in the *Lord Heal My Hurts* Bible study. As I read over the first chapter of my own story I am almost stunned to realize that I have some very good childhood memories and should have had good memories of my teen years as well had I not been so deceived, discouraged and so embittered over all I didn't have. How could I hold on to bitterness if I realized that God had been such an active (and present) participant in the details of my life and in the carrying out of His plan for me?

I am so thankful that by the time my mother became ill and moved into our home that all visible traces of Mara and her bitterness were gone as well. And I'm glad that Pastor Holder had so many opportunities to visit with her and get to know her better. He felt as though she'd had a real change of heart and I have no choice but to believe so myself. There had been too many seeds of truth sown into my mother's life and too many prayers offered on her behalf through the years for me to believe otherwise, especially if I truly take God's word to heart. "So will My word be which goes forth from My mouth; It will not return to Me empty, without accomplishing what I desire, And without succeeding in the matter for which I sent it." (Isaiah 55:11). That accomplishment may not have been made until my mother was on her deathbed but I am only able to envision her entering into heaven and being greeted by Granny, my father, Rhonnie's sweet mother, the babies none of us ever knew and my Heavenly Father.

Of course, Satan's favorite thing about me had always been my lack of self esteem and he'd fashioned many a fiery dart as a result of it. Satan attacks many young women in this area, it seems. It's really odd to me that secondary to low self worth, pride would be one of my biggest problems. I've often said that I really have nothing within myself to be prideful of and I really do credit any real success I've had in life to God's work and His sovereign plan for me. That said, I can't begin to count the number of times I made a bad decision as the direct result of shear, stubborn pride. More times than I can count I had to cover up my real feelings when revealing them might have meant admitting a mistake or an error in judgment. In the past, pride put me on the defensive, caused me to lie to others occasionally and accomplished no good thing in me. "Pride goes before destruction, And a haughty spirit before stumbling." (Proverbs 6:18). No wonder the enemy loves the sin of pride so much.

As a lonely and frightened teenager it was shear pride that kept me from confiding in anyone the remorse I felt over the direction my relationship with Carl was leading. Of course it didn't help that I had no real friends, but I know now that there were people I could have confided in; like the lovely young woman I babysat for and greatly admired. The day I told her that Carl and I were getting married she'd said to me "I've never heard you say that you love him". I remember trying to muster up as much enthusiasm for the situation as possible but I think she knew that I was headed for disaster; definitely an example of pride going before destruction! And I certainly never would have admitted that I'd made a mistake to any member of my family. And let's not forget that prideful list of things I said I would never do once upon a time.

Beth Moore says that pride is the true enemy of ministry; oh how I agree with her. It is only through God's mercy that I didn't come away from my first year of service (if you can call it that) to the women of my church so many years ago in complete humiliation. My response to the Lord's call on my life should have been to immediately begin humbling myself before Him and the ladies but instead the whole notion of actually being elected to 'serve' as their president had gone straight to my head.

It was that very issue of pride that kept me from asking for help from other ladies during that first tenure as Women's Ministries president as well. I could so easily have shared my feelings of inadequacy with Brenda Holder, our sweet pastor's wife, Sandi or one of the other women on the board that year but because of pride I wanted to look like I had it all together. I don't remember even asking God for help that year, at least not sincerely. Pride in that situation often caused me to feel isolated, even a bit resentful at times, yet when new ladies would come into the church I would get so puffed up with pride that I would want to make sure they knew who the WM president was; what a great example of a haughty spirit right before a stumble!

Another destructive byproduct of pride in that instance came when I found myself resentful of the woman who was elected president for the year that followed because she had real vision for Women's Ministries and was so obviously Spirit led and in tune, not only with what the Lord wanted to accomplish, but with the ladies as well. I, on the other hand, was too ashamed to attend ladies meetings for awhile. The Lord has certainly used these areas of service to teach me. He's even used the attitudes, that were so wrong to begin with, to teach me as well. I'm so thankful that He is a God of many chances and if a little humiliation has to precede those second, third and even fourth chances than I am all for it.

But perhaps the most direct assaults of the enemy that I have had to counter have come in the form of greed and envy and I can't even remotely blame my mother for this. This destructive element of my character reared it's ugly head while I was a young teenager. When I mentioned early on that I had to struggle with one of two disturbing character issues from my teen years, in the course of doing some proofreading my friend Gayle was afraid for a moment that I was still boy crazy! I assured her that except for the four grandsons I was no longer boy crazy but that evil spirit of covetousness and greed still likes to rear its ugly head on occasion.

I've spent money I didn't have to buy things I didn't need and even then, for many years was completely unsatisfied with the material possessions I did have; all because of greed and envy. That is very much the nature of material possessions; they don't satisfy and they never will. Only lately, it isn't so much possessions that I envy but the success of others; especially in the spiritual realm. I've learned to weigh this very carefully and I've learned to allow the spiritual success of others to spur me on to pursue the success my Father has prepared for me. "Iron sharpens iron, so one man sharpens another." (Proverbs 27:17). I believe that He wants us to succeed in every work and endeavor He has prepared for us just as we as parents want our children to succeed in the areas where they are gifted. I'm never going to have the same ministry or answers to prayer that others have but I will have the ministry and answers to prayer that my Father has ordained for me.

I don't in any way consider myself to be all grown up and completely together nor do I want to give the impression that I have all the answers but I certainly know Someone Who does! I have learned a few things and one of the most important things I've learned is this: none of my circumstances, situations, trials or problems is unique to me alone yet at the same time we are all fearfully, wonderfully and lovingly handcrafted individuals. Many women I know have expressed feelings of loneliness to me as well as feelings of awkwardness and inadequacy. I know sweet godly women who have been through divorce, suffered the loss of loved ones and have had trouble forgiving themselves for past sins; sins that have long been forgiven and forgotten by our Heavenly Father.

Leading us into sin certainly brings the enemy a sense of victory but he is equally thrilled with the feeling of isolation we sometimes experience when we walk through a tragedy, commit sin or experience failure. I know Satan used my God-given uniqueness to cause me to feel as though no one else could ever understand, forgive or even care about me so I didn't dare let myself be vulnerable and I believe that was exactly my mother's response to every trial or tragedy she faced; she withdrew from the rest of the world so that no one would see how much she hurt or that she needed help.

In contrast to our Father's plan for His creation the devil has a mass-produced plan for all of us and that plan is just for generalized calamity however he can introduce it into our lives. He may use different tactics like substance abuse and addiction or strongholds of ideology for some while for others it might be criminal activity or sexual sin; he'll just keep trying until he finds something in his arsenal that works unless those vulnerable areas of our hearts and minds are protected and shored up through prayer and the knowledge and application of God's Word to our lives.

Another of his other favorite weapons is just plain old garden variety discouragement. During the years when Rhonnie and I battled infertility and the loss of four pregnancies the disappointment was almost unbearable at times and led to discouragement on more than one occasion. I am so glad that we committed that area of our lives completely to the Lord very early. I have no regrets or lingering disappointment over those losses because I trust my Father's sovereignty completely. Disappointment is a natural reaction to something unpleasant in our lives but if we let him, Satan will use it to form other weapons he will then gleefully use against us. Disappointment left unchecked can lead to discouragement, bitterness, anger, greed and pride.

It's so important to know what Satan can and can't do if we are going to battle him effectively. When Rhonnie and I were trying so desperately to have a baby more than one person made reference to the devil "stealing those babies". I've always had difficulty swallowing that concept because I don't believe he has the capability to snatch away something that is so fearfully and wonderfully made and protected. I firmly believe that God has a plan for each and every one He creates and it is God who numbers our days, not the enemy but the enemy did use the disappointment and the grief that I felt over the losses to steal my joy in the Lord and any strength I might have derived from that joy for a time. I've learned to be careful what I give Satan credit for but I'm sure he derived great pleasure from the fact that others believed that he might have been responsible for those losses.

Finances are another area where we often blame Satan either for over-our-head indebtedness or loss of money through bad investment or unwise spending. We are called upon to be good stewards of what God blesses us with whether it is spiritual gifts, talents or material blessings and when it comes to finances I believe that Satan has called out legions like never before in view of the major credit card debt crisis that plaques our society today. His hand is all over that but he has not been able to steal anything from me in this regard that I willingly (and greedily) handed over to another.

That brings me to a couple of other weapons that Satan uses regularly against God's creation. Along with overspending I have occasionally turned to overeating when I'm stressed instead of turning to the Lord. The devil enjoys every minute I turn to cheese fries or chocolate instead of God because he knows I won't find any answer or comfort in those things. God is the only one who can bring me joy or give me peace. When I make myself unavailable to minister to the needs of others because I just don't want to be inconvenienced Satan likes that too and he's happy to take the credit. We must identify the enemy and know his tactics before he can be dealt with effectively. He hates God and rises up against Him through His beloved creation every chance he gets!

Along with correct teaching on the Holy Spirit I would have benefited a great deal from some fundamental teaching on dealing with the enemy after my initial salvation experience. Lessons on spiritual warfare were sorely lacking in my early discipleship though I believe this was more through oversight than intention. Had I been properly discipled I would have received some good old fashioned basic training for the inevitable warfare while I waited for the Holy Spirit to fill me. I would have then been both empowered and equipped for the inevitable attack that would come my way. Instead I was completely ignorant regarding the enemy's wiles.

I had weaponry available to me that I didn't even know about so I sure didn't know how to use it. And I naively thought my old vulnerabilities had completely vanished when I gave my heart to the Lord. During those first couple of years I tried to do what I knew was right but I was doing so in the 'power' (or lack there of) of my own might and I have the battle scars to prove it. I've since learned that there is only one way to fight this enemy and the instructions for effective warfare are clearly given in God's Word.

I wish I'd been told that I would face an enemy whose fury had once been a bit subdued but now that I'd taken a stand for the Lord he would come at me with full force. Most every lesson I ever learned in life has been learned the hard way and what I learned about dealing with the enemy has been no exception. Early on I said that I had no intention to give the devil more credit than he deserves and this chapter is not about him; it is about our rights as Christians and about the resources we have available to us. It's about recognizing and being informed about our enemy and his tactics. He's our Father's enemy too and it is only through the Holy Spirit that we are empowered to deal with him effectively.

I know my enemy and his strategies and I also know that every time I've said to him "I will resist you in the name of Jesus" he has fled; every single time. When I don't submit to my Father either with an outburst of anger or occasional pity party I'm joining the ranks, however briefly, of those who speak wickedly against God; that realization usually gets me in line very quickly. Remember, sometimes Satan's darts are difficult to vanquish, especially when the flesh gets in the way, but possible because of 1 John 4:4. "You are from God, little children, and have overcome them; because greater is He who is in you than he who is in the world."

When the seeds of fear, anger and low self esteem were being sown into my young life Satan was watching with rapt approval. He knew I would do anything to fit in and he gave me lots of unhealthy options. He loved it when I entered into a covenant that I would one day break because he knew the house Carl and I were building was being built upon the sands of lies and deceit. He had been the architect of that house, lies and deceptions happen to be a couple of his specialties, and he was pleased that the feeble house would not withstand the storms already brewing on the horizon.

Satan was certainly gleeful when greed and a spirit of covetousness were introduced in my teen years and when roots of bitterness came up, just as he had ordered later on. He had to be salivating over all the wrongdoing I willfully entered into after I had committed my heart to the Lord and the icing on the cake for him was that I took others along with me. "Do I not hate those who hate You,

O LORD? And do I not loathe those who rise up against You? I hate them with the utmost hatred; they have become my enemies." (Psalm 139:19-21-22).

I am certainly still very much a work in progress; I probably battled a little seed of discouragement like you wouldn't believe just yesterday. I wanted to indulge in a real worm-eating, no, forget the worms and just pass the chocolates and the tissue, pity party! Why he absolutely loved it and I'm sure he felt as though he was the guest of honor. What nerve!

Everything the enemy does is motivated by his hatred of our Lord and of those He loves and that is what we, as God's people, need to always remember about him; that and the fact that he has already been defeated. Knowing that his days are surely numbered he's out to destroy the Lord's creation however he can but here is the good news. "The LORD your God is in your midst, a victorious warrior. He will exult over you with joy, He will be quiet in His love, He will rejoice over you with shouts of joy." (Zephaniah 3:17). The victor is in our midst and He not only created us with a plan and a purpose He loves and rejoices over us. I know I can stand against God's enemy and mine with complete confidence and that makes me want to shout for joy!

Chapter 10
The Everlasting Way

"Search me, O God, and know my heart; Try me and know my anxious thoughts; And see if there be any hurtful way in me, and lead me in the everlasting way."
(Psalm 139:23-24)

I can't believe that I have just chronicled all but the last few years of my life and oh, have these last years been eventful. Among other things, about four of those years have been spent writing this book! In 2001 Christopher married Erica, the girl we had all fallen so in love with on our very first meeting and five months later he graduated from Southwestern. That summer they moved to the Chicago area so that Erica could attend Wheaton College in pursuit of her master's degree. Then, a year and a half later, they had their first fearfully and wonderfully made child, a little boy; the fourth grandson for doting Grammy and Grampy. Soon afterwards the family moved to San Antonio, Erica's home town (and one of my favorite places to visit) then back to the Chicago area and then to Boston. Christopher and Erica seem to want to make sure Rhonnie and I always have a place to travel.

The turn of the century would also bring some surprises, much needed renewal and the resurrection of my long lost dream to write, teach and minister to women in a most unexpected way. In January of 2000, just a little over a month after my mothers passing, New Life Center held its annual business meeting. That evening a proposal was made to sell the church building and to relocate. There were a number of major and costly repairs that would need to be made to the building and a developer had offered a large sum of money for several properties in the area. It seemed to most to be the best solution for what had been a mounting problem through the years. There had been talk of selling and relocating a few years earlier but this time tempers seemed to flare and when all was said and done the difficult decision was made to sell and rebuild our church as soon as possible. As a result many were hurt or angered and immediately left the church.

The following Sunday it seemed that half the Women's Ministries leadership as well as a deacon or two were missing and the remaining deacons and their wives were asked to stay after church for an emergency meeting. While the men were meeting at one table the wives gathered at another and Brenda asked us all if we would take positions on the Women's Ministries board. She would lead the women herself if we would all help in whatever way we could. I, of course, had not attended a ladies meeting in quite some time but now that I no longer had my fulltime job or my ailing mother to care for I had already fully intended to become active in Women's Ministries again, I just hadn't foreseen becoming quite so active so quickly. Still, I wouldn't have considered saying no to Brenda's request even for a minute because we were all reeling from the reality of what had just happened to our church and we were all determined to do as much as we could to see our pastor, his wife and all who remained faithful to New Life Center through this difficult time. Though it was a real trial for our church it was also a time of real bonding for those of us who remained.

Until that Sunday meeting my biggest plan for this next season of life was to finish the redecorating and painting projects we'd begun before my mother became ill. I believe that for several months the front of our house was one color while the sides and back were another. The only other thing I had on my mind for the immediate future was the highly anticipated Disney cruise that Rhonnie and I had scheduled for the end of March. (It was fantastic – like a second honeymoon!)

I was totally unprepared for what happened next when Brenda asked me if I would consider leading a ladies' Bible study that spring. It's odd, because even though I had truly not expected the question I know that the Lord had been preparing me for it because I didn't even hesitate to answer "yes" and in fact in that very moment something awakened in me that I had put so far out of my mind that I scarcely thought of anymore but I knew almost in that instant that I would soon be writing and teaching and even ministering in a way I hadn't imagined before.

What made the entire conversation so completely remarkable is that up until the mass exodus of some very hard workers and precious people Brenda would not have even thought to ask me to teach a Bible study. She said that she'd been praying about starting a daytime study for several weeks and had someone else in mind to lead it but that lady had been one of the first to object to the planned move and was no longer available. How is that for a door that had previously been locked up tight suddenly swinging wide open? It swung so widely that it almost hit me in the face! On the way home that day my husband had rather a long face but I was so excited I could hardly stand it!

Almost immediately the wheels in my head began to turn. I really didn't have to think too long about what I would suggest we study in the spring. When I prayed the very first thing that came to my mind was the Kay Arthur study *Lord Heal My Hurts* that had meant so much to me years before. The Lord was laying ground work for this book by refreshing my memory of that study and the impact it had on me. He also began to speak to my heart about my role in leadership both alongside my husband in the deacon ministry as well as on the women's board. In the past I'd not taken either role very seriously but as God dealt with me about His plans for my future I knew I would have to give my all to both ministries if I was going to fulfill His plan and His calling. God was preparing me to lead the women once again and for the next several months every time Brenda spoke of making changes to the women's board after our move was complete He confirmed it to me. I felt I had real purpose at New Life Center for possibly the very first time.

Several women signed up to take the spring Bible study, *Lord Heal My Hurts* and I led another study in the fall of 2000 and yet another in the spring of 2001. In the fall of 2000 we'd broken ground for the new church that would be just a couple of miles from our home in Broken Arrow and New Life Center seemed to be filled with a sense of anticipation. I was enjoying leading the Bible studies but was growing a little restless teaching material others had written; not because I thought the material was lacking, far from it, but I felt an increasing desire to write a study that I could present to our ladies and finally in the spring of 2003 I was able to lead my own Bible study, entitled *Always in Season* on the fruit of the Spirit. The study was well received by the ladies and that lead to the writing of two more studies but I kept feeling I should be writing something else altogether. I began to sense that God was speaking to me about my own platforms for ministry and for sharing my testimony so I sat down to write that novel about the wise and wonderful teenaged girl who found the Lord when she was at a most precarious point in her life.

I thought about this for about a year and when I finally did begin the story I found that the writing was ridiculously slow-going. I was a little surprised by that because I was not having trouble imagining the story at all. Imagination has never been a problem for me, and I finally attributed my writing difficulties to all the things that were happening in our lives what with all the trips and moves and babies, etc. In spite of my vivid imagination, I was, for the most part unproductive where the novel was concerned and now I realize that the writing of it just felt awkward.

Maybe it was because I had reconfigured the character that I called Julie so much that I didn't know her at all. I'd rewritten the first couple of pages so many times I was starting to write and rewrite the same things over and over again. After writing for about a year I still had not produced even the first chapter of the book I was writing. I just couldn't shake the feeling that I might be missing something crucial.

As I sought the Lord I began to gradually realize that He was telling me in that still, small voice of His that I needed to tell my own story in autobiographical form, not fiction - sugar coating or rewriting all my mistakes, but honestly and openly telling my life story, my own and very real testimony of all the situations and circumstances He'd brought me through. (The Lord wanted me to tell the real story not a made up version of it.) I really didn't want to do that so I dragged my feet for another good little while and I found the fact that I was now leading Women's Ministries at New Life Center a very convenient reason to procrastinate. Another convenient excuse was provided in the fall of 2004 when I began a new career as Mothers Day Out teacher at New Life Center's preschool. In addition to having some very good excuses to put off my writing I also genuinely wondered who in the world would want to read about me.

I began to sense that the Lord was giving me material for another writing; the devotion book for woman that had been my original desire but I now understood that I couldn't write another thing until the book He was directing me to write, this book, was finished. I wondered what my husband would think about the telling of our story and what Andy and Jennifer would think about the events that both led to and ended my marriage to their father. I just wasn't sure I had it in me.

One Sunday morning during worship I began to feel such a sense of shame and embarrassment because I knew I was supposed to be doing something very specific and yet had found every excuse in the world not to do it. I was either too busy or too distracted or all those old thoughts of inadequacy would creep in and I was still honestly wondering who in the world would want to read a story about all the sin and the failures of someone they didn't even know. Of course, I knew the focus would not be the sin and folly but rather the power of God in my life and no one would ever realize that, not even me if I didn't begin to act in faith and obedience and that very day I told my Father that I would write my story and that when I finished the writing it would be His to do with however He pleased. If somehow you are reading my story today I believe it is because He has chosen to use it in your life in some way.

Within a few days I scrapped poor Julie's story and began to write my own. I wish I could say that I breezed through the writing of it like there was no tomorrow but the truth is that there would be many tomorrows before I even began to feel like I was making progress. I bathed the writing in prayer and seemed to come up with some very good things to say, that is until I sat down to actually write them. Then it seems my mind would go almost completely blank. I would write furiously for days on end, and then weeks would go by when I wouldn't write a word.

All this time I don't think I'd told anyone what I was doing except Rhonnie and a couple of my preschoolers. They were very supportive; especially my husband, that was one obstacle completely removed, and the preschoolers promised they wouldn't tell a single soul (it was helpful that at less than two years of age they could barely talk). I wanted to tell a couple of others too but I knew that I would only be able to tell a select few; people who I could trust to pray with me and to hold me accountable. After much prayer I felt directed to tell Mary Read one of the older saints in our church who has been one of my prayer partners for years and my friend Gayle;

and again both were extremely supportive, even a little excited. Gayle volunteered her editing skills on the spot (and she gave me a printer to use when ours 'fizzled out').

I eventually told Pastor Holder who was also very supportive and now I knew that I would have to get very, very serious about my story that I was now absolutely certain God was directing me to write. I would need to work and not just talk about it and amazingly the work was now easier because I knew that I had good, solid prayer support from some very precious friends. When I gave Andy and Jennifer the first three chapters I knew by their reaction that I had their approval and support as well. I would now be the only one that stood between me and the telling of my story.

Philippians 1:6 says something absolutely vital to me; "For I am confident of this very thing, that He who began a good work in you will perfect it until the day of Jesus Christ." I knew at that point also that if the writing of this book was truly God ordained He would help me see it through. I know now why the writing of the novel was a futile effort; He had not ordained that book or that story, at least not at that time. I've learned to say the verse with the word 'me' in place of the word 'you'. "For I am confident of this very thing, that He who began a good work in ME will perfect it until the day of Jesus Christ." If other books are to follow they will come in His ordained timing and for His ordained purpose as well.

My Heavenly Father continues to amaze me and soon after I began to write in earnest I 'reminded' Him that I wanted to have a more intimate relationship with Him. A few days later I was excited about the future and my pursuit of this deeper relationship. As I got into my car to head for preschool that morning when I reached for my seatbelt I found I had accidentally closed the car door on it so I opened the door just enough to retrieve it. As I pulled at the seatbelt the door closed all by itself and very hard on my left hand. It hurt so badly that I felt pain all the way to my elbow; I couldn't grasp the steering wheel and a large red bump immediately arose on the top of my hand. I actually thought for a moment that it might bleed, and though miraculously the skin wasn't broken I was afraid that a few bones might be. At the very least I expected a horrible bruise to be visible for a very long time.

Sitting in the driveway, I began to cry and my first thought was "why, Lord, would you let this happen to me today, of all days, I prayed this morning and I was ready for the day, how can I drive to work, how will I pick up babies, how am I even going to be able to stand this pain?" Rhonnie was in the house and I started to get out of the car to see if he would pray with me and quite frankly I wanted a little attention and some good old fashioned babying but the Lord stopped me short so I just sat in the car and prayed. I asked Him to touch and heal and to do a complete work in me because in addition to the pain I was also just a little angry.

Almost as suddenly as the car door had closed my hand stopped hurting and I was able to back out of the driveway and head toward the church. Before I had driven a block I realized that I had just had an incredibly intimate moment with the Lord. When I had asked Him twenty years earlier to help me relate to Him as Father I believe that he did that in a very significant and meaningful way but it still wasn't the way I normally related to God. What I realized in that moment in the car was, that like a child would do, I had run to my Father, He'd dropped whatever He was doing to scoop me up and comfort me and to do whatever was in His power to make it better. What was in His power was to completely heal my hand in an instant. What's more, He wanted me to run to Him so He could show me His love all over again. Throughout the day only the smallest red mark remained and there was never a bruise or even a hint of pain. I was so overcome by the shear intimacy of the experience that I couldn't talk about it for several days.

It wasn't the healing, awesome as it was, that had overwhelmed me so. It was the way my Father dealt with this child; He gave me the attention I needed in that moment and even the babying that I wanted as well and I was reminded of the childhood memory I have of my natural father picking me up and lifting me high in the air. At some point during the day I remembered that I had reminded the Lord that morning that I wanted a deeper and more intimate relationship with Him and this is what my heavenly Father gently spoke to me. "Isn't a Father/daughter relationship much more intimate than creator/creation?" From that day forward my way of approaching Him was drastically altered once again. I believe He wanted to remind me that morning that I am my Father's child and that everything He has done for me in the past He will continue to do all my days. He will continue to hedge me in, order my steps and when I cry out to Him He'll answer.

More recently I was blessed to have an opportunity to share my testimony with my New Life Center ladies for the very first time. In the past I'd shared bits and pieces on an individual basis as the Holy Spirit has directed but never had I been so real and so open with them about my past. It was my coming out of the woodwork party. I told them that night that if I could stand before them and say in all honesty that I have a good marriage, a blessed marriage and a truly happy marriage - anyone can!

I'd once invited a lady to come to one of our women's functions and in an effort to convince her that I really wanted her to attend I told her that among other things, our ladies meetings are always such a good opportunity to get to know each other a little better. She laughed and said "if you get to know me better you might not want me to come back". I assured her that would never be the case. After all, New Life Center ladies allowed me to come back and I've been coming back for over twenty five years. I promised this dear woman that if they would not only let me come back but that they would welcome me with open arms anyone would be welcomed back again, and again and again!

I explained to my ladies that if I could live righteously before them (remember, we walk by faith and not by sight) anyone can! Just look at what He brought me out of! If I could be actually used by the Lord in ministry; to lead the Women's Ministries, teach a Bible study or lead the Sunday morning prayer class – anyone can! And most important of all I told them that if I could have a personal encounter with God, indeed, if I could call the Creator of the universe Father – anyone can!

The 139th Psalm is still as meaningful to me today as it was so many years ago when I first studied it and I hope through this scripture and my own life experiences that others will also realize how uniquely and wonderfully God has had His hand upon their lives. That is the whole purpose of the sharing of this testimony; so that others might be able to see what God can do.

Looking back, particularly at my childhood, my fire years and most especially the years after I was first saved when I experienced the most intense onslaught of Satan's wrath, I remain amazed in the knowledge that God knew everything about me, and He knew it intimately. Yet, in spite of the wrong path I was taking, He refused to abandon His plan for me and the works that He had prepared beforehand for this daughter. Though I was traveling a path that did not bring Him honor and glory, He made sure that the path would not lead me to destruction.

He knew my ugliest thoughts and heard every angry, hurtful word yet, once again, He enclosed me in such a way that Satan was never able to get close enough to destroy me. Truly that knowledge is too incredible to comprehend. Even after completely rededicating my life to Him I often allowed the past to prevent me from being all I could be in Him. He turned those painful parts of the past that threatened to keep me from fully serving Him into something that He could use. He taught me to forget the 'what ifs' and 'if onlys'. No one can rewrite the past, not even God but He is able to redeem it and because of that redemption I have a life that once seemed out of reach because He also knew my hearts deepest desire and even when I abandoned that desire He did not. I can't imagine what the future might hold but I can't wait to see what my Father will do next!

    I still feel an occasional twinge of shame when I think of the years I made my bed in Sheol, knowing I had not escaped my Father's presence even there. I had never wanted to live in such a place; it just seemed to be the only place fitting for me for a time. It certainly wasn't the place I wanted my Father or even my mother to visit. I'm awed and humbled in the knowledge that my Father watched as carefully over the lost and confused young woman perched by the grave as He once watched over the little girl in the swing. But I've also found that when I think I'm in a good place I tend to be less aware of His presence. Sadly I'm also more inclined to neglect my time with my Father when all is well but still He remains there, diligent and attentive, with His powerful right hand laid hold of me. It has become my desire to bask in His presence in both good times and in trials because I now know I will never be anywhere that His Spirit cannot go.

    I will forever be amazed at how in my darkest hour, the days when I thought that my marriage to Rhonnie was over, He was there and when I cried out to Him He instantly intervened. I'd cried out in desperation to my Father through a prayer that I'm fairly sure I hadn't really expected He would answer. Instead, He performed a complete and life-changing miracle restoring not only my marriage but my relationships with my children and mother as well. He was also there to comfort me during four miscarriages, the death of Rhonnie's sweet mother and my own mother two years later as well as the regular disappointments and ups and downs of life. He's been my light in the darkest of places.

I no longer wonder if the verses in this Psalm are out of order; nothing in God's Word is ever out of place and I also know that there is nothing out of place about the plan that He sovereignly and uniquely designs for each and every one He creates. He knows the end from the beginning in all our situations and circumstances. He even planned that those awkward and lonely feelings that I once experienced would all play a part in the woman I am today. Yes, I did eventually learn to turn being different into an art form but I still experience pangs of awkwardness and isolation on occasion but now I know that most everyone else does too at times and because of my own experiences I can relate so much better to the feelings of others.

I am absolutely in awe of the notion that my Father thinks about me all the time. Isn't it sad that we live in a world that wants nothing better than to distract us and keep us so busy that our time with the Lord is hurried or often non-existent? One day as Gayle and I were praying the Lord had given her a verse during her devotions that morning that she shared with me during our afternoon prayer time. It is such a precious verse that I wanted to just bask in it. "The eyes of the Lord are toward the righteous and His ears are open to their cry." (Psalm 34:15).

As I meditated on that verse I got a picture of our doting and attentive Father watching and listening intently so as not to miss a single thing His child might say or do! I'm saddened that my thoughts toward Him are not as all consuming nor are my eyes and ears as tuned in to all He is saying and doing. Oh, am I ever still a work in progress! I still occasionally get sidetracked even doing work that He has ordained and I sometimes still try to do His work while operating on my own steam yet His thoughts toward me outnumber the sand and as soon as I cry out to Him He hears and He's there.

I've learned who the enemy of my soul really is. Pride, anger, bitterness, greed, envy, discouragement, loneliness (isolation) even feelings of inadequacy and awkwardness are just weapons he's formed against me. The enemy delights in using those feelings to keep us from being everything we were fearfully and wonderfully made for. I know this first hand because I saw it in my mother and I very nearly traveled that same road. It is also a fact of life that spiritual warfare will ever be a part of life on this earth. I'm so glad this enemy has already been defeated. I believe I have a powerful testimony because God has worked powerfully in me and for me as He has brought me through my life's own particular circumstances, hurts and joys. Truly, I can say to Satan just as Joseph did to his brothers "As for you, you meant evil against me, but God meant it for good in order to bring about this present result..." (Genesis 50:20). The enemy's attempts to bring evil against me have resulted instead in platforms for ministry so that God might be glorified!

God is always searching, always knowing and always, always, always leading us in the everlasting way if we will only follow. He's been doing so ever since He formed us in the womb. "Search me, O God, and know my heart; Try me and know my anxious thoughts; and see if there be any hurtful way in me, And lead me in the everlasting way." (Psalm 139:23-24). This has become a daily prayer of mine. I know when I'm really open to knowing my own anxious thoughts or hurtful ways I am much more careful how I think and how I approach and respond to others. He wants to help His children deal with anything within our hearts or minds that might prevent us from being fully His.

As long as I draw breath my own story remains unfinished, only these chapters are written because my Father alone knows what the future will hold and only He has penned the ending. I look forward with great expectation to see where He will take me and to see who will cross my path. My Father always knows best! As a child I had a dream but never a goal or even a plan for realizing that dream and for the most part I really had no hope for the future because my hope was only in the temporal or in whatever I might be able to achieve on my own. I thank God that He had a better plan that would give me much more than I had ever imagined. Amazing!

And even though this particular story is mine, it could have had anyone's name on it because in the end it isn't a story about me at all it is a story about God's love, His protection and His plan for those He loves. We are told to "Remember the former things long past, for I am God, and there is no other; I am God, and there is no one like Me, declaring the end from the beginning and from ancient times things which have not been done, saying, My purpose will be established, and I will accomplish all My good pleasure…I have planned it, surely I will do it." (Isaiah 46:9-11).

Did my Father allow me to make my bed at the edge of Sheol for a time so through my redemption others might also be able to visualize theirs or the redemption of another young woman living dangerously close to the grave?

Did He bless me with an amazing husband, wonderful children and grandchildren as well as a large extended family so I could see how He has more than filled my life with all the things I craved as a child? It's so much better than the *Father Knows Best* family I once idolized because this family is real and just as my Father tailored it.

Did He plant me squarely in the midst of an amazing church and bless me with godly friends so my life could serve as an example that no matter who you are or where you've been your past does not have to be a forerunner of your future? I certainly believe that He did!

And what about the hardships, disappointments and trials I've faced? Platforms for ministry, of course, but they are much, much more than that. The greater ministry is that I not only have survived them but that He has brought me through each one knowing that He loves me, will never desert me and so that others can look at those hardships and know that He can do the very same thing for every one of His children if they will allow Him to.

One of the most valuable life lessons I have learned is that God will always act according to His Word. From the moment we were so fearfully and wonderfully woven in our mothers' womb our Creator has known us and has thought about all the ways He would make Himself and His plan known to us. He's made plans that we should know Him and love Him and be used mightily in the work He's tailored for us from the very beginning. The sovereign and holy God of the universe has personally watched over our every step as He's protected and nurtured us. He's known our every thought and heard our every word because He's never left our side. Our Deliverer has defeated the very enemy of our soul and has equipped us by His Holy Spirit for victory as well. And most important, our every life experience, both good and bad, has been designed to draw us into our Father's arms; we were designed to know Him in a personal and intimate way.

I know dear women who are struggling to keep their marriages intact and their families together as they pray for an unsaved husband. There are precious mothers, dear friends of mine, whose children are in rebellion, perhaps feeding from the pigs' trough or sleeping at the edge of the grave; I pray they know there is hope for them. There is hope for the one who is lonely and for the one who feels awkward or different. And there is hope for the sinner who feels unworthy of God's love because of past mistakes and here is the proof. "He has not dealt with us according to our sins, nor has He rewarded us according to our iniquities." (Psalm 103:10). He's our Father and His love for us is as certain as the dawning of each new day.

I'm so thankful that my Father has not dealt with this daughter according to what I deserve. I am so blessed and I know that He loves me and that He has never once turned His back on me. He's forgiven me for often taking His lovingkindness for granted and for doing my own thing my way, even when I knew that His way was better. I am so thankful that my Father has lavished blessing after blessing upon this once poor, misguided and miserable creature. He's merciful beyond comprehension, His grace is sufficient and He cares for His creation.

Even as this story draws to a close my Father has begun the writing of a new chapter and a new adventure is on the horizon; one that surely will take me to uncharted territory and will draw me even closer to Him. I can hardly wait to see where He will take me and how He will use me and I can't wait to tell about it because I see another platform for ministry already being built and I gladly give Him the honor and the glory for all He will do.

"Now to Him who is able to do far more abundantly beyond all that we ask or think, according to the power that works within us, to Him be the glory in the church and in Christ Jesus to all generations forever and ever. Amen." (Ephesians 3:20-21). If anyone can ever say that she is blessed beyond measure and loved beyond her wildest dreams I most certainly can because this is exactly what He, the one I call Father and the one who knows best, has done for me.

Made in the USA
Lexington, KY
25 May 2011